Recipes
for
Life

Recipes

for

Life

A Cookbook for the Heart and Soul with Edie & Friends

Edie Hand

Foreword by Vestal Goodman

PELICAN PUBLISHING COMPANY
Gretna 2000

The word "Pelican" and the depiction of a pelican are trademarks of Pelican Publishing Company, Inc., and are registered in the U.S. Patent and Trademark Office.

Cover design: Denise Fussell
Cover photo: Billy Brown Photography
Interior Design: The Font Shop

ISBN 1-56554-860-4

Manufactured in Canada
Published by Pelican Publishing Company, Inc.
1000 Burmaster Street, Gretna, Louisiana 70053

Unconditional Love Recipe

Remember, Son, if you're a success,
I would be as happy as can be.
But remember, too, that when you fail,
You can always come to me.
There's little in life we cannot share,
We'll share the bad times, too.
For my love has no conditions, Son,
That's what I give to you.

*I dedicate this book to my son, Lincoln ("Linc") Addison Hand.
Thanks for just being you and allowing me to always be me.*

*"I am love. Love has no limits, no boundaries, no
conditions placed upon it. It is there, rich and free, for those
who possess Me. There is no charge in My love, no vacillation,
no end. This is the love that follows you all the days
of your life, the love that engulfs you, that satisfies
all the needs and desires of your heart."*

Snapshots from TNN's
"Holiday with
Family & Friends"

Carolyn and Buddy Killen
checking the script

My son, Linc, with
Miss Alabama 1999, Julie Smith

Me with Sister Schubert

A room full of friends

Racing legend and great guy
Bobby Allison

Buddy Killen and me with Jessie Colter
and her husband, Waylon Jennings

(left to right)
Producer "Speed Racer,"
Rick, Tennessee Governor
Don Sundquist, and Bubba

Marty
Raybon and
the kids in
"Christmas
Comes Alive"

*C*hallenges certainly presented themselves in September 1999 when I decided to produce the television pilot based upon *Recipes for Life*.

The result was "Holiday with Family & Friends: The Real Recipes for Life" which aired on TNN (The Nashville Network) during prime time on Saturday, December 4. The program originated from the home of my long-time friend and fellow Alabamian Buddy Killen, who not only agreed for me and a television crew to take over he and wife Carolyn's home for nearly a week, but "my" Buddy also said he would host the show with me! What a guy! From Friday to Tuesday, professional decorators from *Southern Living*'s Oxmoor House Book Division, as well as Birmingham's "Anything Grows," all merged at the Killen Estate to give it a Christmas touch . . . in October, that is!

It was no easy task. Finding the delicate balance between holiday decor and at the same time keeping Buddy and Carolyn's house their own was priority number one! And their house looked great.

I wanted the television show to reflect the main theme of this book, which is—live your life to its fullest extent by cherishing what I call my "Eight F's." In the show we used four of them—Faith, Family, Fun, and Friends. These are my recipes for life. For faith, I invited my great friend, Vestal Goodman, who not only blessed us with her recipe for life, but sang a heartfelt rendition of the Bing Crosby classic "White Christmas," per-formed as only Vestal can! Buddy invited his close friends Jessie Colter and her husband, Waylon Jennings. Both treated us to a moving rendition of "Silent Night," which not only our audience loved, but had our crew teary eyed as well! These generous two gave us their entire evening on what was their 30th wedding anniversary! After the show, both Jessie and Waylon commented how much they enjoyed the spiritual side of a holiday cele-bration, even though Waylon himself admitted he only learned one Christmas song in his 40-year career! That song was "Away in a Manger," which he shared with the entire roomful of guests during our taping!

Speaking of taping, this was an unconventional television show. Not once did we address the camera like it was an actual program! Instead, we decided that this was going to be a *real* party, with the television audience as invited guests. This presented some production challenges, but in the end, we gave TNN a show unlike anything that has ever aired on CBS Cable before!

I'm so happy my dearest friends, Dr. Judy Kuriansky, Darlene Real, and

Roxie Kelley agreed to take part in an on-air toast to our long-term relationships as compadres. We rolled up our sleeves in the kitchen with baker/entrepreneur Sister Schubert, touched upon the many wonderful accomplishments of The Susan G. Komen Breast Cancer Foundation through a heartfelt chat with Chairperson Linda K. Peterson, and witnessed firsthand the triumphs of a close-knit family currently battling the disease. My sincerest thanks to the Allen Family, Jeff and Tammie, and their two sons, Aaron and Ryan, for pouring their hearts out so that others may be strengthened and inspired by their story.

We had the first interview with Tennessee Governor Don Sundquist, or "The Gov," as he said I could call him. The Gov was a great sport, and actually agreed to a little comedy bit our writer added that had Tennessee's top legislator competing with Julie Smith, Miss Alabama 1999, in a friendly game of video football. Wouldn't you know it, Alabama beat Tennessee! (Just for fun of course.)

Special guests also included the multi-talented Ronnie McDowell and his son Tyler, and Florence, Alabama, native and MCA recording artist Alecia Elliott and her family. Both Alecia and Ronnie went above and beyond the call by staying late two nights in a row! Muscle Shoals native Marty Raybon blessed us with his talents on both nights as well. Graciously accepting our invitations to the party were: Kalyn Chapman, Miss Alabama 1993 and Visionland of Alabama Spokesperson; The Christmas family (mom, Candy, and daughter, Jasmine); the multi-talented Ben Speer and Otis Forrest; and all the parents whose children stayed up way past their bedtimes to be part of the show!

The television show was about family—and someone who I consider family is stock car racing legend Bobby Allison. He opened his heart and soul as both he and I discussed the losses of loved ones. He lost his sons, Davey and Clifford, and I lost my brothers, David and Phillip Blackburn. All died tragically at young ages in accidents.

For me, the television show was a lifelong dream come true. Have you ever had a moment in your life that you cherished so much and at the same time wondered how great it would be if you could share it with the ones you love? That is what "Holiday with Family & Friends: The Real Recipes for Life" was for me. Not only did I have the opportunity to celebrate a spirit-filled Christmas, but to be able to share the entire event with a national television audience was a moment unsurpassed in my professional career. Cheers to everyone involved who made this project a reality.

Thanks go to my TNN friends, David Hall and Brian Hughes, who gave me the green light on this unconventional project; to my business partner Ben McKinnon, executive director of the Alabama Broadcaster Association; to my great friend and fellow cancer survivor, Alabama state senator Roger Bedford; to Frances Smiley, director of Alabama Tourism; and The Tennessee Film and Music Commission, who helped make this television show a reality. Special thanks to Roxie Kelley who was my encourager and my "rock," and to my sister Kim and my nieces Kristi and Kayla Poss. Last but not least my son, Linc. My little boy has grown into a fine young man with a great future ahead of him. Thanks, Son, for not only your contribution to the television show, but for your unwavering support throughout the years!

Contents

broadcasting my radio show!

Foreword

*E*die knows the power of prayer. God's healing touch has been proven time and again in her life and battle with cancer. When the storm was raging, Edie's faith in God became her peace.

Her family left a great heritage of gospel music. Although her cousin, Elvis Presley, was known as the "King of Rock 'n Roll," the only awards he won were for his first love, gospel.

When Edie walks through the door, sunshine fills the room. Edie Hand's love for the Lord is that ray of light. Her strength and pure joy inspires everyone who knows her. Edie is never a stranger long because wherever she goes the friends she makes are forever.

More than just great recipes, the book will encourage and strengthen your faith in God. Darlin', I believe that Edie will bless your life as much as she has blessed mine as my friend.

—*Vestal Goodman, "Queen of Gospel Music"*

My dear friend Vestal Goodman

Susan G. Komen "Race for the Cure" 1999

The Susan G. Komen
Breast Cancer Foundation

1·800 I'M AWARE

One of the most difficult experiences that I have encountered throughout my lifetime has been my twenty-year-long battle with various cancer threats. One of the most devastating types of cancer I had to deal with was breast cancer. Early detection is the key to surviving this disease. Thanks to medical technology and my regular checkups, including mammograms, the doctors were able to discover the cancer in its earliest stages.

Perhaps one of the greatest warriors in the battle against breast cancer is Nancy Brinker. Ms. Brinker established the Susan G. Komen Breast Cancer Foundation in 1982 to honor the memory of her sister, Susan G. Komen, who died from breast cancer at the age of thirty-six. Ms. Brinker is not only special to me because of her efforts to combat the disease that has been a part of my life, but also because she and her sister share another common bond with me. All three of us are members of Zeta Tau Alpha Sorority. We have never met, but we share the same ideals and purposes set forth by the organization. I am a member of Zeta's Eta Rho Chapter at the University of North Alabama. Our philanthropy is breast cancer awareness and we work with the Susan G. Komen Foundation.

Credited as the nation's leading catalyst in the fight against breast cancer, the Susan G. Komen Breast Cancer Foundation and its powerful grassroots network continue to break new ground in the battle against the disease.

The Foundation's mission is to eradicate breast cancer as a life-threatening disease by advancing research, education, screening, and treatment. Tens of thousands of volunteers in more than one hundred communities nationwide work through Komen affiliates to further this mission through awareness and education programs and various fund-raising events. In addition to funding major national research initiatives, the Foundation delivers the lifesaving message of early detection to hundreds of thousands of women and men through innovative community outreach programs.

The Komen Foundation has a National Toll-Free Helpline, 1-800-IM AWARE, which is answered by trained, caring volunteers who provide timely and accurate information to callers with breast health and breast cancer concerns. In addition, the Foundation's award-winning Web site (www.breastcancerinfo.com) provides visitors with up-to-the-minute breast health and breast cancer information, as well as the latest news from and activities of the Komen Foundation.

meeting President Bill Clinton

One of the greatest singer/songwriters ever! The late Tammy Wynette backstage after a show at my alma mater, Red Bay High School

Acknowledgments

One of the greatest things that has come out of writing this self-help cookbook is my new friendships. My interns, Melanie Hargett and Sunshine Schumate, became collaborators in their unfailing support of this project. They not only spent hours typing recipes and attitudes, but these young women contributed their journalistic and public relations abilities in dealing with my famous and soon-to-be famous friends.

To my special friend, Dr. Judy Kuriansky—I want to thank her for always being able to bring out the best in me and for giving so graciously of her time and energies.

I appreciate Vestal Goodman for her many talents and her witness for God. Thanks for including me in your family of friends. You are the darlin'!

Many thanks to my friend Ellen Riley, and a personal thanks to her husband and my business associate, Jim Riley. Without Jim's recipes for living sanely, I would not have been able to meet all of my deadlines.

I want to express a special appreciation to Ben Speer and Mark Aldridge for their efforts and encouragement. To Cherina Rice, isn't editing fun?!! To my neighbor Jody Schefano, for teaching me to enjoy the art of cooking gourmet.

I really appreciate the contributions to this book from all of the staff at Cumberland House, including publisher Ron Pitkin. I especially want to thank Tom Spychalski for all of his efforts and the Font Shop staff for helping me achieve my goal.

This book, as most of my projects are, is a team-work effort thanks to the Susan G. Komen Foundation, Zeta Tau Alpha Sorority, and the University of North Alabama, my alma mater, and the friends of American Women in Radio and Television.

Thank you also to Darlene Real for helping to select the cover colors and my wardrobe, Billy Brown Photography for always bringing out the best in eyes, John Croyle and the Big Oak Ranches, Bill Gaither, Willie Smith and family, Buddy Killen, Brenda Russell, Dave Koz, Dolly Parton, Marlo Thomas, Carol Anderson, Roy Clark, Ralph Emery, Ann Sward Hansen, Sister Schubert, and Dr. Patrick Daugherty.

I want to thank all who shared their recipes for living a fruitful life, and I thank you for sharing your heart and soul so that others may be inspired to find the right ingredients for their lives.

The Gracies 2000 in New York

Edie with Kathy and Mark Fable
of Quinn Fable Advertising

Linc Hand with event host of "Gracies,"
Kathie Lee Gifford

Recipes
for
Life

Introduction

*M*y kitchen is a place that offers me great peace, fun, and, often, reflection. One evening, I was buzzing about trying to figure out what to make for dinner. I didn't have time to shop that day, so I knew I would have to "wing it." As I opened and closed cabinets looking for things to put together to eat, thoughts of other parts of my day ran through my head. There was business (my book deadline, a report due, and an important meeting), family (my son's upcoming visit, my father's illness, and my sister's home burning to the ground), and other interests and responsibilities (a church fund-raiser, the song I wanted to learn on my new piano, the friends I needed to call). As I took out various foodstuffs and condiments I could put together to make something edible, the similarities between preparing this meal and organizing my life merged. I smiled as it struck me, *here I am, creating a new recipe for something to nourish me, when all the other thoughts in my life follow the same concept, feeding other parts of my being.*

At the table, looking at the salad I had improvised out of leftovers, some canned goods, and some fresh vegetables, I reflected on how I could combine the other aspects of my day to be equally appealing, as well as nourishing. And what are those important elements? They all turned out to have names that start with "F." They include: Family, Finances, Fitness, Food, Friends, Faith, Fun, and Future. These came to summarize what I now hold dear, the "Eight F's" that comprise the ingredients of my "recipe for good living."

In reflecting on my life, I'd have to admit I have been through many joys and many tragedies that a great number of you can relate to. You will read about my experiences as I have told them to my dearest friend, loyal confidant and counselor, Dr. Judy Kuriansky. Basically, I've lived the lifestyle of an average Southern mother and businesswoman, but I've also been blessed with extraordinary experiences and exceptional friends and family. Through my life's travels, I have been privileged to meet many wonderful people—some famous to the public and some just to their loved ones—who also have been through compelling experiences. In talking with them, I realized their stories, too, have been wondrous ways of putting together the Eight F's to create their recipe for life.

Throughout this book, I offer you stories of the experiences of other wondrous women and men, as well as my own experiences, that you may read and find inspiring so that you, too, can reflect on your own recipe for living.

Family

My sister Kim, with her daughters Kayla (front) and Kristi

What words immediately come to mind for you when you hear the word family?

For me, the words are love, bonding, and commitment. Those are feelings I have shared with my son at this stage of my life. I appreciate my parents and the qualities that they instilled in me, the efforts they made to create a warm household, and the caring and support from the extended family of close friends I have.

But things weren't always that way.

There were parts of my growing up that would fall under the ever-so-popular words of the 1990s—dysfunctional family. Reflecting back (though without blame or regret), I see that I took on the role of mothering my other siblings, therefore giving up a part of my own childhood. I was focused on thinking that it was my place to be a mother hen gathering around her chicks (my siblings) to take care of them.

Later, as I grew to be a teenager, I added to my thinking the feeling that I had to earn a living to take care of the family. Though my father, of course, worked, I still felt I had to mind the other children—and even my parents. I carried this caretaking and controlling too far, even into my marriage, creating some dysfunction there. Admittedly, I mothered my husband and even mothered some friends.

Today I realize there is a healthier way to be part of a family. I still provide love and support, but I also allow others to take responsibility to care for themselves and carry out their share of the responsibilities.

Recipes require the right amount of any ingredient. I have also learned a better balance in my life between the ingredients of family and work. Admittedly, in the early days of my career, I put way too much time into my work at the expense of not spending time with family. I have often apologized to my beloved son, Linc, for that (and fortunately he has forgiven me). Today I deal with family differently. I don't feel I have to drop

My second cousin Elvis, while he was stationed in Germany

Elvis' grandmother and my great-aunt, Minnie Mae

Me with my three brothers, Phillip, Terry, and David

Edie's grandmother Alice Hood Hacker

everything to take care of fixing others' lives or to continue allowing destructive family dynamics or relationships in my life (more on one of these major disappointments in a later chapter). I have evolved to know that I need also to take care of myself; that, truly, when you love yourself, you are able to love and take care of whoever you call your family in a better way, and be a part of their lives without necessarily caretaking.

I have come to accept the problems that emerged during my youth because my parents did not know how to be there for me when I really needed them. Now, even though they never were my best friends as I might have hoped, I have come to a place of loving and appreciating my mother and father for who they are in their golden years.

I have also come to accept the problems that emerged in my marriage. There were times that I either tried to control my husband, as I did my family, and times I let them control—and hurt—me. Now that my ex-husband and I divorced, we have a more mutually respectful relationship.

I now have a relationship with my son of which a mother can only dream. In the early years of Linc's life, because I was rarely home, he spent more time with my husband's family. Much as I had always wanted a child and loved him with all my heart, I could never express it the way I really wanted to. I just didn't know how to give him what he needed, just like my parents didn't know how to give me what I needed. Then, too, my marital problems made me drown myself further and further in work, my health problems made him fear he would lose his mom, and therefore he had to cling more to his dad.

I am lucky I got another chance with my son. Now Linc and I snow ski and travel together. He came with me to Washington, D.C., and met Vice President Al Gore, our Alabama Congressman Tom Bevill, and President Bill Clinton,

my son, Linc Hand

who has invited me to bring Linc to the White House again so that he may show us both his Elvis collection. I go Linc's to college to watch him play basketball and get the greatest joy from just watching him talk with his friends. I pray that he can get through his anger towards me and what he's seen from his father's demonstrative style of dealing with life's issues, and I trust that he has the mature mind to forgive the past and change the negatives to positives.

My experiences with my son have made me see that if you could sit down and realize that whatever you are feeling from the pain it is not worth what you do to another human being you love. If you don't really sit down and reflect or seek counseling to find yourself, you will end up missing something great in your life because there is nothing more special than the bonding with your own flesh and blood. Do something about it instead of saying you wish you would have, could have, should have.

My thoughts return to the happy experiences of my family in my childhood—the days of family picnics at my grandparents in northwest Alabama with aunts, uncles, cousins by the dozens, and an occasional visit by Elvis and Aunt Minnie. It was literally "all day singing and dinner on the ground," but I know there was also whiskey in the bushes. Grandma would say, "The devil's all around." Even so, Grandma Alice was praying with her hands upraised to the heavens asking God to protect and save all her family.

The deep love I feel for my brothers and sister carry me through my darkest hours. God knows they have suffered. Two of my beloved brothers died so young and so tragically. But even beyond the grave, their spirit is still with me. Another brother has lingered at death's door with a brain aneurysm (more of that story later in the faith section). My sister, her husband, and their precious two daughters are an intimate part of my life and my recipe for family and love.

Most of all, I have learned to make time for family within the context of the rest of my life—my work, friends, time alone, and of course, for my God (more about that later in the section about faith). As my faith has become stronger, I find time to give selflessly to the people precious to me, with God helping guide me to where I need to be.

Now I am ready to create a healthy family, like a healthy hearty meal. I have that with my son, Linc, and I am ready now, more than ever, to have that with a loving mate, whenever such a man comes into my life.

Food

"*Luscious Elvis*" Red Velvet Cake

I am an incurable romantic when it comes to food and dining. I love a wonderful place setting. I love the food placed on the table looking inviting. To me, it's truly a symbol of giving and receiving love.

What are my favorite culinary delights? You might call me a simple Southern lady. I love hot tea with lemon and honey! I love grilled chicken with rice, a caesar salad, a baked sweet potato, corn, and yogurt with fresh strawberries. Also, I love going out to dinner with friends and having a special gourmet meal. We will include gourmet dishes, as well as simple home-style cooking and heart-healthy dishes in the following pages.

If someone prepares a meal for me, I feel loved. But I have also learned to extend that love *from* myself. If I am eating alone, I make it pretty for me. I put my nice placemat out over a lovely tablecloth and light a couple of candles while dining on my fine china.

My grandmother Alice taught me that I was special and that if I always treated myself special, then I would be.

Today so many families eat on the fly, but when I was growing up, it was a time for family to sit down and eat together. I remember dinners together. Mother was a good cook whose talents always made wonderful aromas of sweet baked potatoes or chocolate cookies flow through the house. It was Grandmother Alice who taught me to use fine china, to love hot tea, and to enjoy buttermilk biscuits with chocolate gravy for breakfast. Bless her heart, Grandmother raised 12 children, 55 grandchildren, 18 great-grandchildren, and 6 great, great-grandchildren on those staples!

My grandparents lived in a large white house with white columns and a wraparound front porch nestled on hundreds of acres. I grew up in a tiny community called Burnout, Alabama, a typical small rural area just like you would see in the history books, with white fences and white houses and rolling hills with ponds. Our home was a lovely colonial brick house sitting in the center of forty acres with Indian mounds on the property. It was a great place to grow up with my siblings. My brothers and I would alter the sign entering Burnout to read, "Burnt Plum Out," because, believe you me, there was nothing exciting happening in Burnout except on Saturdays when Mr. Elliott would slice bacon at the local grocery store. Grandfather Walter was a farmer and a lumberman. My paternal grandfather, A.L., was a contractor and my grandmother Floy was a dietician in the little town of Red Bay. She lived to serve her family delectable meals and I was taught to tow a strong work ethic and enjoy a good meal after a hard day's work.

Edie's maternal grandfather Walter Hacker with uncles Ace Hacker, Reynon, and Wayne

But that importance went astray as I became a wife, young mother, and businesswoman with no time to spend on what I had grown up appreciating. Throwing together something to eat became the habit at mealtimes, instead of focusing on careful selection and spending quality time together. Many times I even forgot to eat, being so caught up in my business day, writing, producing, and running to meetings.

And now I have come full circle, back to my roots. I have partly refocused on the role of food in our lives because of my health. What you eat becomes that much more important when you have experienced bad health. With all the pills and medications I had been taking for years for all my various illnesses, I could not eat many things, and had to learn to eat smaller meals more frequently to keep my body energized and ward off migraines.

Now that I have overcome some of these health problems, I am focusing on foods of my childhood. I see the value of caring about food for continued health, but also I see the preparation and service of food as a joy to be shared with others. For this reason, I have concentrated on these practices and foods for better health in the cookbooks I have been writing. Sharing the recipes with others has given me a renewed connection to my roots and to my loved ones. Through my own experiences and those of my special friends, I feel sure you and your tummy will enjoy the recipes for life that are offered in this book.

Friends

Friends have always been a treasure to me. They are like jewels in a crown. My grandmother told me when I was little that friends were like our flower garden. You should only select the finest rose or lily or whatever flower you want. I still cherish that. There is nothing better than having a beautiful bouquet of "flowers," or friends to share memories with as we travel down life's road.

To have a good friend, you have to be a good friend, as the saying goes. I live by that saying. To be a good friend, you learn to give pieces of yourself to those you truly love.

I have been blessed with close friends throughout my life. They are truly there for me through thick and thin, through fun and horror. My sister has always been a best friend, and still is to this day. Your friends offer support, will offer whatever resources they have when you need them, and love you unconditionally. That is what Dr. Judy has offered me through all these years. My closest friends have also worked with me on projects, like Roxie, Ann Sward and Dr. Judy, who appear, on my TV shows (for free when I need them), or do lectures or appearances for whatever

My closest friends (left to right): Darlene Real, Roxie Kelley, and Dr. Judy Kuriansky

women's shows or mall fairs I am producing. They are there for me through my deepest, darkest times. Those who last a long time are a wonderful record of your history, like Debbie Lustrea Pausch (whom I call a prayer warrior), who was in my wedding and there through both my brothers' deaths, as was Peggy Rice Mitchell, a college friend. Judy Hester Bodie and I grew up together and were roommates after college and still

Me and Rochelle in London, clowning around

stay in touch. Then there are newer friends who are like sisters because of our bond with the Lord, like Judy Sargent and Rochelle Brunson. To me, they are like the song "Friends are Friends Forever."

I have also suffered disappointments and loss with some friends. A Birmingham friend, Darlene Real, and I were very close, until she went through changes in her life (including a divorce) and felt that I didn't give her what she needed. Though I had many regrets and sadness over this loss, I had to come to realize that we each had different needs at different times and simply misinterpreted each others actions on various occasions. We have renewed our friendship. Another major disappointment was with my cousin, with whom I had written a book. A project that I thought would bring us together instead tore us apart, leaving me devastated for a year. I am sure everyone can understand what this is like. For many agonizing hours I explored this experience and resolved it by finally turning it over to God. By following God's way, we are always working towards healthier relationships. In relationships, sometimes, others' attitudes and actions toward certain circumstances are misinterpreted.

One lesson I learned is that expectations can lead to disappointments. Have a goal, but be open minded to the attitudes and opinions of others, for we all look at situations through different eyes. Trust in your friends, but be prepared that sometimes your heart may be broken. Cherish those friends who celebrate your happiness and devote yourself to their happiness.

Faith

There have been several nights I have been alone with a little candle, wondering what purpose I serve on this earth. Then my answer comes—one person can make a difference!

I have dedicated my life to making the lives of others happier and more fulfilled. I realize that if God gives you the charisma to bless others, then it is His gift and His light to you to be used for His glory. In my life, every day now, I give Him all the honor and glory for whoever I am.

I am filled with so much appreciation for God that it spills over to every person in my life. The lesson here is that there are not enough hours in the day to call people in your life and tell them what they mean to you. Every moment counts, for we truly never know what tomorrow will bring.

My life now is enriched by faith, but how did I come to this point?

I grew up as a Southern Baptist in Alabama. My faith has been through evolutions, and I must admit I have not always followed the exact guidelines. I believe that God allows us to make adaptations, as declared in the Southern Baptist teaching "once saved, always saved." The guidelines of my childhood prohibited drinking, smoking, and dancing. But I loved theater and cheerleading and did these things despite the teachings. Those acts made me feel guilty for many years, but now I have come to realize those actions were between God and myself, and I no longer need to punish myself out of fear. Religion helped me develop good morals and character as a fundamental way of life, but I always felt different. Rather than torture myself for this, I have come to see that God created us all differently for a purpose. I am His servant and must embrace my difference as He embraces me, and all of us.

Crises have changed my life and deepened my faith to bring me to the point I am at now. It is astonishing to me to find that I have the increasingly unique experiences of "angels" being present in my life. It's likely they have always been there, though I was not aware. They come in the body of friends who may call me out of the blue with a kind word or a gift when I need it most. Or they come in a spirit that overcomes me in my quiet moments when I am meditating and communicating with God.

Sadly, I grew up looking outside of myself for happiness, instead of listening to that still, quiet voice of God within me. Now I do that and I have come to realize I can do difficult things.

Out of my faith I have forgiven many who have hurt me and realized that out of my greatest pain has come my greatest growth.

For many years of my life, I didn't feel whole. Because of the pain and abusive experiences I was subjected to, I became detached and withdrew into those different personalities some of us recognize within ourselves in order to be able to survive. I was pulled in so many directions that I didn't know who the real Edie was. There were even times in my darkest hours of despair when I was so tired and frustrated, and physically ill (I even spit up blood from the cancers in my body), that I didn't think I wanted to be alive anymore.

And I felt lonely after my brothers' deaths, a painful divorce, the betrayal of certain friends and business partners, and later, suffering the empty nest. When my son went away to college I cried for six weeks.

It was too much for me to handle, and I wondered what was the purpose of my going on. But my faith, even as fledgling as it was then compared to now, kept me going. As a Southern Baptist with a Pentecostal background as well, I was taught that we don't question God, we just keep going. I thought if I just worked harder, it would get better.

For years, I pushed at doors to get a book deal, a TV show, a top-title corporate job, and it happened, but there were doors that closed. Now I see why certain doors closed; I was pushing at doors, but I was pushing *my way,* not God's way. Now I have developed a deeper sense of faith so that I have given my life up to God, for His plan, not my own. I learned much from this lesson in the *Experiencing God* workbook by Dr. Henry Blackaby and Claude King used by my Sunday school class at Shades Mountain Baptist Church in Birmingham, Alabama. The course allowed me to find my real goal and purpose in life, "which is what God wants and not what I want." This has helped me to be better in all the "F's" throughout this book and to meet all the challenges in my life as a better person.

People hear my long list of tragedies: my divorce, my brothers' deaths, many illnesses

I was head cheerleader for the Red Bay Tigers my senior year in high school, 1968-1969

and operations, and wonder how I got through it. "Where did you get the strength to go on?" they ask. I have learned that my strength was from God. He has given me the courage to go through my brothers' deaths, special family members' deaths, and my brother Terry's battle for his life. I remember the day my sister, Kim, and my mom, with other family and friends, drove Terry to UAB in Birmingham, Alabama, to have brain surgery. The day was dreary and filled with anxiety for all. Terry had asked me to hold a solid gold horseshoe pendant for him. He said, "Edith, please keep this for me. I want to give it to someone with a pure heart and I will let you know who." I agreed to his wishes. The time came for his moment to travel to surgery on that cold stretcher. The look of terror on his face is etched in my mind. I was with him talking until time was no more. I promised, "and a promise is a promise," to go to the chapel in the hospital to pray until he was safely in his room. I told him I would saddle up a horse with him and we would start to swim the lake at home. I knew I'd meet him on the other side, but if something happened I'd be there to help him with his crossing to meet God. I was on my knees in this warm setting, totally with Terry and God, when Terry's "horse" got in trouble. It had been only four hours into a twelve-hour surgery, and I knew something was terribly wrong. I rushed to the nurses station. The nurse said, "Ms. Hand, I was about to come and get you. The doctor needs to see you, your mom, dad, and sister, only, in the conference area." I hurried to get them. The news from Dr Fisher was painful. He said, "I have failed Terry because the aneurysm is too deep in the brain and I have cost him his hearing on one side. If I don't go back in within the next twenty-four hours to relieve the pressure, he will die today." My mother and father slumped over and wailed like babies. My sister was devastated. I could not speak. After witnessing the scene of the room I asked Dr. Fisher Terry's chance for a normal life if he even survived the night. He could give no answers as tears streamed down his face. I asked if we could see him.

The best way I can describe the room where Terry lay was like entering a war zone. There were burn victims, individuals with no limbs, and much moaning and faces I will never forget. My brother's face was one of agony. He had a shaved head cut from one end to the other with a hole left open and was given nothing for pain because of the next surgery. His hands were tied down and so were his feet. Blood was going in one arm and IV of fluids in the other. He screamed, "Edith, help me." I touched his face and wiped away his tears as I fell on my knees to ask God to intervene.

Left to right: sister Kim, Edie, brother Terry, and mom Sue

Terry said, "I know now what Jesus felt like when he was nailed to the cross." My sister's heart and mine were broken for him. I asked if I could stay the night with him. They agreed because I think they thought he wouldn't make it. Terry entered the next surgery but it failed, too. I was with him through the night and helped the nurse with his body's needs. Later the next day, when he was stable, he looked over at me and asked if I had the horseshoe necklace. I said, "It's here Terry, on my cross necklace I have around my neck." I asked him what he wanted me to do with it. Terry's words and actions touched my heart and changed something in me that day that is hard to explain. He said, "My dear sister, I want you to keep my solid gold horseshoe because you have always taken good care of me and you have the purest heart of anyone I know. Wear it and tell my story when I am gone." I have it and wear it often. You see, Terry's faith and courage have kept him here on this earth longer than any doctor predicted. He doesn't have the quality of life he would like but he wants to see his two sons graduate from high school. It has been four years now, and they graduated in 1999. God is faithful to those who believe.

God has been my special friend, beside me all the way, helping to make me the person that I am today. He is my guide for the day, He is my partner, my lover, my husband, my child, and my comfort. He is the ultimate cook, designing the recipe of my life, as He is doing for many others as well.

Feel those angels around you—as I do—and realize they are the messengers of God come to help you. And you, like me, will never feel alone again.

Fun

Though, as I have shared with you so far, there have been many tragedies in my life, there has also always been fun. It has been my saving grace, along with friends and my faith.

My fun comes from simple things. I can have fun driving down the highway, cooking up a last-minute dish, practicing on my new piano, and even cleaning my barbecue. I can have fun doing anything—and so can you. My friend Roxie Kelley has been my partner on many fun "scenes of crime." She is my "Road Warrior Queen." Whether I am travelling with her to Gaither Homecoming Shows or

Dr. Judy and I co-produced and hosted Total Wellness for Women

seminar presentations, we have found constant laughter. (You will hear more about these experiences in a story under this section of fun.)

Fun comes from feeling free, free to be yourself, and free of others' judgments. I recall the days of doing the TV show *Total Wellness for Women* with my cherished friend Dr. Judy Kuriansky. She would fly down from New York to be with me to produce and host the series about all aspects of women's lives (everything from addiction to healthy cooking) that aired on stations throughout the southeast in the mid-1980s. In the mayhem of writing the segments, booking the guests, and putting together all the necessary elements of a talk show, we were frantic, getting up at 6 A.M. and rushing to the studio. What was fun? That we would bolt out of bed, jump into the shower, and then dash into the car and drive the hour to the studio with wet hair (mine in curlers) and our bathrobes! There we were, going through the drive-through for a greasy fast-food breakfast, wildly tossing papers, planning, and laughing.

What better example of the joy of abandoning yourself to fun than on a recent trip to London with some of my Sunday school pals, when our group went out to have dinner at London's Hard Rock Café. We enjoyed waiting in line by dancing in the streets. We dined on hamburgers, fries, and shakes, and we lost all sense of age by throwing straws and even putting some up our nose! There we were, all respected and respectful women, allowing ourselves to be little girls again.

Fun started for me as a child. I picture myself in panties, a little top, and pigtails, picking my teeth, sitting on a bench with my two precious brothers, waiting for the mailman to come, laughing as we noticed amusing things about people who drove by. We could laugh about how a lady named Ruth would drive by, with her kids hanging out the window, and she'd be smoking a cigar. It looked like something out of a comic strip. We would nickname these characters—laughing with them, not at them, for we were country kids, too.

Fun comes from always being a child. I love riding bumper cars, I love swinging in the park, having a picnic, eating an ice cream cone, and walking on the beach.

Fun comes for me by living a similar lifestyle to the character Lucy from the TV comedy, *I Love Lucy.* I love giving people pet names, particularly calling them "Ethel" or "Louise." Later, I myself would have a pet name, after the character Pearl, developed with my one-time advertising partner, Jack Voorhies, a great humorous writer in the South.

I am proud, now, to bring out the kid in others. In the last three years that I have been developing these cookbooks, I see clearly how I have fun watching other people enjoy their life. Even simple observations can give great joy. Just the other day I got great joy from watching my nieces clasp my son's hands as we went to the movies. And I get great joy from my son show me the muscles he is developing from working out. I get a kick out of asking Kayla, my six-year-old niece, how much she loves me. Her reply is "99,000 times I love you," and one evening I asked her three times, and her final answer of the evening was, "I told you three times, Aunt Edie, I love you 99,000 times. Is that not enough?" Precious moments in time!

Don't let yourself miss those small moments of fun. Life is the most precious gift

Edie with Waylon Jennings during the TNN taping, and on our flanks are radio personalities Rick & Bubba

in the world and we all are running too fast. Don't let the music run out before you get to dance. Drink and eat the fruits of your life more often. In two columns, write down where you are today, and where you would like to be. But before you just yearn for the latter, enjoy the former.

Fitness

I never made an effort to be fit. Running around with a thousand things to do was always my "exercise" for the day. That seemed to be enough. It certainly worked when I was younger and I didn't have to "work at" my body. I also never focused on looking beautiful. Even though I won beauty contests in high school and college, these victories were not real affirmations to me of, "Gosh! You've got it!"

Years later I was to have a rude awakening. I developed a series of very serious illnesses that seemed to drag on for years. Every year there was another frightening diagnosis, a series of tests, and a regimen for getting better. Often the doctors were unsure of my fate and the news was ominous. I took an endless amount of medications, all of which created other complications and problems. The drugs and the increasing stress from life and from the illnesses caused me to put on at least thirty pounds. Even worse, I couldn't think clearly. This turn of events was my wake-up call to begin paying more attention to my body, as well as my lifestyle.

I was scared through many of my operations that I might die. In fact, I thought I would die. I guess you could say that the light went on in my head about the importance of being fit when I realized that to prepare to die gracefully, I had to begin to live fully. My principle for the next twenty (or more) years that I hope I have to live is that if you prepare to die, you prepare to live harder, with zest, seizing ingredients, and looking and feeling your best.

A fitness program requires mixing exercise with eating right. Every morning I do my stretching and exercises, but also follow with a regimen of vitamins. I hope that this combination will eventually replace any medications I still take. I have become more health conscious.

In the senior years of my life now, I care about being fit, not just for my physical health, but for my emotional health. As I enter this new stage of my life, I am interested in having a mate again. That has given me an extra incentive to feel good about myself. Everyone needs to find the motivation that works.

Now, I may be stressed (as we all get in life), but I deal with it differently

than years ago. I have
learned that you become
healthy when you know you
are loved for you, when you
believe that you are pretty
on the inside, and when you
know you have God in your
life. If God overcame the
world, then not one of us
would have any problems we
could not overcome. I
believe with all my heart the
message of Psalms 37:4,
"Delight in the Lord and He
shall give you the desires of
your heart."

*Edie with "Gomer and Goober,"
Jim Nabors and George Lindsey*

Being totally fit helps
you achieve a sense of peace and reduce stress. Here are my ingredients for
that: sharing with positive people, listening to music that soothes me,
writing down my thoughts and feelings, walking on the beach, and watching the sun rise or set. A new ingredient I've just discovered is appreciating the things in my own backyard (literally and figuratively)—that means
walking in my yard and looking appreciatively at my home. I even enjoy
looking in the mirror and finally liking who I see looking back at me.

Finances

The road to financial freedom begins not in a bank or even in a financial planner's office, but in your head. It begins with your thoughts. I
believe financial freedom is something we all strive for. I am trying to be a
better steward of my money. First, I discuss my finances with God. I set
goals for my short-term needs, then I plan for the long-term. Being a single, working mom, I have had my share of pitfalls along life's journey, but
I have learned no problem is impossible to overcome. Take charge of your
destiny and achieve financial freedom. Keep in mind to focus on your goal,
not money, and the money will come. I believe Zig Ziglar—he says that
when you help someone else achieve their goal, you will achieve yours. My
friends who are financial planners will share their tips and attitudes for the
right ingredients to set you free throughout this book. I will also share

with you my thoughts on how to be a good mentor and network your way through life.

Future

There are two messages I would like everyone to get from the excerpts of my life story and from this book of recipes contributed by many people.

One is my favorite saying from Helen Keller—"When one door of happiness closes another opens, but if you stare too long at the one that's closed, you'll miss the one that's opened." This makes me seize every moment in my life.

The other is the famous parable from a story about Christ. Suppose you are facing problems in life, and feel deserted by God. You say, "At times Lord, I know You have been there for me, because I have seen Your footprints next to mine." But then you ask, "This time, Lord, in my darkest hour of trouble, I look down and see only one pair of footprints. Have You abandoned me?" And the Lord answers, "No, those footprints are mine. I am carrying you."

The lesson here is that the Lord never leaves you. You are always in His sight and in His arms. You are never alone.

Remember this as you face putting together the ingredients to your life. This will help you make the best recipe.

I rejoice in your "cooking up" the best for yourself and your loved ones!

And remember, whatever you do, faith and right motives will reap the best reward for you and all mankind (and womankind)!

> *It is the very business of your life to cultivate every faculty you have, in the belief that He has given them to you that you may become His instrument for his usefulness.*
>
> —THEOPHILUS PARSON (1797–1882)

Edie with, to left, Linda Peterson, chairman of the board for the Susan G. Komen Breast Cancer Foundation, and to right, Tammi Allen, breast-cancer survivor and her family during the taping of "Holiday with Family and Friends, Recipes for Life"

We should all adopt the legend of the unicorn as a philosophy of life. The legend states that the unicorn was a beautiful creature that lived on the earth for a short period of time. It brought peace, love and prosperity to everyone that is met. The unicorn ultimately died of a broken heart because of all the evil in the world. We are only on God's earth a short period of time. Let's try to bring peace and happiness to those we meet and not hate and anger. And if we believe in others as God believes in us we might eliminate some of the evil that exists in our small corner of the world.

—Joyce Thompson Heames
professor, Samford University, Birmingham, Alabama

I talk to the Lord all day as I go through my daily routine. I start the day by putting my concerns or thoughts for the day in a diary, and then I read scripture and consult with the Lord on each of these things. This is where my peace comes from. When my mind has self-condemning or outgoing negative thoughts, I try to stop them because I know that they are not from God. I have learned that God can take care of every part of my life and He has led me to happy and fulfilled living.

—Judy Sargent, Birmingham, Alabama

Judy Sargent and me on the Gaither
Homecoming Cruise (I was recovering
from my lumpectomy)

*In New York with
network producer Darcy Bonfils*

My recipe for success is to start each day with expectations for success and happiness. Each day, I try to live life to the fullest, giving work my all, in performance and conscientiousness. I give my heart to my friends and family, my humor to make the sun shine in my life, and my hope for the best that life has to offer.

—Darcy Bonfils, ABC producer, New York City

Linc with rising country singer Alecia Elliott

Starters

Down Home

Frisky Fruit Salsa

1   cup pineapple chunks
    (fresh is best), reserve
    ½ cup of the juice

½   cup mango, cubed

1   medium orange,
    coarsely chopped

½   cup green bell pepper,
    coarsely chopped

½   cup red bell pepper,
    coarsely chopped

½   cup lime or lemon juice
    (lime is preferred)

¼   cup fresh cilantro,
    chopped

1   teaspoon paprika

1   teaspoon chili powder

In a saucepan, mix all the ingredients. Bring to a simmer. Simmer 5 minutes, cool, and refrigerate. Salsa is best when allowed to "set" overnight—that way, the flavors mix quite nicely.

Makes 6 servings

Christine Wilson, Jasper, Alabama

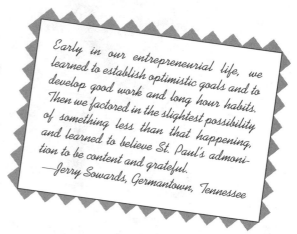

Early in our entrepreneurial life, we learned to establish optimistic goals and to develop good work and long hour habits. Then we factored in the slightest possibility of something less than that happening, and learned to believe St. Paul's admonition to be content and grateful.
—Jerry Sowards, Germantown, Tennessee

Heavenly Ham-Filled Party Biscuits

½   cup butter or
    margarine

1   3-ounce package cream
    cheese, softened

1   cup all-purpose flour

1   cup baked ham, ground
    Brown sugar
    Dry mustard

In a bowl, cream the butter or margarine and cream cheese until light and fluffy. Stir in the flour with hands until thoroughly mixed. Form into a ball, wrap in waxed paper, and refrigerate 1 hour or so before rolling out. Roll out dough into a rectangle about ½-inch thick. Sprinkle with ground baked ham. Dust lightly with brown sugar and dry mustard. Roll up jelly roll fashion; chill. Preheat oven to 400°. Cut the roll into 16 slices and place on a cookie sheet. Bake for 15 to 20 minutes. Serve hot.

Makes 16 servings

Gina Nichols, Jasper, Alabama

Make Everyone Smile with Salmon Balls

1   15½-ounce can red salmon
1   egg
1   cup corn flakes, crumbled
    A pinch of salt
    Salad oil

Remove the bones and skin from the salmon, than place the salmon in a medium mixing bowl. Crack the egg into the salmon and add the corn flake crumbs and salt, mixing thoroughly. Roll into balls about the size of walnuts. Place on waxed paper.

In a saucepan, heat 1½ inches of oil until very hot. Drop the balls into the oil and cook until golden. When done, remove the balls from the oil with a strainer and cool on a plate covered with a paper towel.

Makes about 15 to 20 balls

Edie Hand

Salmon Croquettes

1   16-ounce can salmon
1   medium onion, chopped
1½ cups saltine crackers, crushed
2   eggs, beaten
¼   cup self-rising flour
    Oil

Remove the skin and bone from the salmon, and place salmon in a mixing bowl. Mash the salmon to separate it slightly. Add the onions, saltines, eggs, and flour, and stir until well blended. Form the mixture into balls in the palm of your hand, using about 2½ ounces of mixture for each ball.

In a deep-fryer or skillet, heat 1½ inches of oil. Drop the balls into the oil and fry until brown. Drain in a colander or on paper towels.

Makes about 8 to 10 croquettes

*Betty Jo McMicheal, Irondale, Alabama,
co-owner, Whistle Stop Café*

How to Decorate a Party Table

1. Get seven yards of gold lamé fabric.
2. Arrange fabric in a swirl on the table.
3. Elevate any dishes by putting cracker boxes under fabric.
4. Provide a fresh flower or plant centerpiece.
5. Use flat and old natural Easter baskets for chips and crackers.
6. Line the baskets with colored cloth or theme napkins or handkerchiefs.

—Diana Bender, Florence, Alabama

Baked Brie and Pastry

Brie, any size
1   17-ounce package
    Pepperidge Farm flaky
    pastry sheets

Preheat the oven to 375°. Wrap the Brie snugly in the pastry sheets. Bake until the pastry is puffed and slightly brown.

Serve immediately on a platter with a cheese knife. Surround with crackers and fruit.

Harold Bradley,
Nashville, Tennessee,
president, Nashville
Music Association

Buddy and Carolyn Killen

Buddy Killen's Favorite Mushrooms

1   8-ounce package fresh
    mushrooms
¼   cup butter
1   teaspoon garlic salt
1   teaspoon pepper
1   teaspoon salt

Wash the mushrooms and let drain until as much water has been removed as possible. In a cast-iron skillet, melt the butter and add the mushrooms remaining ingredients. Cook over medium heat, stirring frequently, until the mushrooms are very brown.

Makes 4 to 6 servings

A few years ago, Carolyn and I used to spend a lot of time on our boat during the weekends, and I remember once when I was just sort of puttering around in the kitchen and decided to fix a batch of mushrooms for our guests. Next thing I knew everyone there was raving about this simple little recipe. It seemed that our friends always enjoyed them so much, so I went ahead and put them on the appetizer menu at my restaurant.

Buddy Killen, Nashville, Tennessee,
owner of the Stockyard in Nashville—ranked among the nation's top 25 restaurants

Buddy Killen's Attitude for Life

Your pre-conceived ideas can keep you from creative thinking and exploring unlimited possibilities.

∼

After being around Buddy Killen for just a short time, you begin to feel his compassion for his fellow man and his zest for life's adventures.

Buddy says, "The journey is more exciting than the arrival. Doing whatever it takes, day in and day out, is the exciting part. Get up with the attitude that you are always searching. Otherwise you are just waiting everyday for the sun to rise and set. Are you preparing to die or are you preparing to live?"

Buddy's story of his rise to success is like so many others. He grew up during the Depression in north Alabama. His family did not have any money, but, despite this adversity, they found a way to enjoy what they did have—each other. As Buddy grew, his spiritual beliefs developed through the fire and brimstone sermons of Southern preachers. He started out with one initial set of ideas, then swayed toward another, and then finally found the soul within his own soul. "Judge not, that ye be judged."

Buddy told his family at an early age that he would, one day, play on stage at the Grand Ole Opry. His youth was spent like everyone else's—there were youthful pranks, but his youth was spent mostly just learning life by living it.

He made his commitment to music at an early age, and although it was unknown to him at that time, every move he made would guide him toward this passion. His story is of a journey characterized by no money, thumbing

friends

for rides, and relying on the generosity of others. Above all, it is about not quitting.

"When the fate, luck, and hard work all pay off, and the opportunity first presents itself, it is not usually recognized for what it is. However, one day you look up from your work and you are the owner of your own company, Tree International Publishing Company." Tree was the top country music publisher of all time. Buddy had made it, starting with Elvis Presley and "Heartbreak Hotel" and moving along with country greats like Bill Anderson, T. G. Sheppard, Dinah Shore, Dolly Parton, Dottie West, and Ronnie McDowell.

The adventure for Buddy kept moving on. In January 1989, he sold his company to CBS, but he stayed on for a while to help manage it. He then decided to focus his attention on Buddy Killen Enterprises. This included Buddy's Stockyard, one of the nation's top 25 dining facilities, Soundshop Recording Studios, and KMG Records, a Christian record label.

Buddy has never lost his one true passion, which is music. He has produced his own CD, entitled "Mixed Emotions." He continues to write and publish songs for all to hear and enjoy. At the right are a few verses that, in a way, tell his story.

friends

I've met the Master on my knees
Been tested, yes, and tried.
I've seen the God of Heaven paint
The fields and countrysides.

I've learned enough to make it through
Each day that passes by
But when I've learned enough to really live
I'll be old enough to die—
Old enough to die.

I'm just a plain, hard working man
No stopping place have I found.
Although I'm tired, I'm still inspired
At night when I lay down.
I've learned to like it on God's earth
And yet I wonder why
But when I've learned enough to really live
I'll be old enough to die.

This is Buddy Killen and a lot of the rest of us.

Lobster Bisque

3   tablespoons butter or
    margarine
¼   cup onion, chopped
3   tablespoons all-purpose
    flour
1   tablespoon fresh parsley
    Dash salt and pepper
2   cups milk
1   cup chicken broth
1¼ cups fresh or frozen
    lobster

In a large pot, melt the butter and sauté the onion over low heat until tender. Stir in the flour, parsley, salt, and pepper. Cook until bubbly. Stir in the milk and chicken broth. Bring to a boil, stirring constantly. Stir in the lobster. Bring to a boil, then reduce the heat and cook for 3 minutes.

Makes 4 cups

Carlene Sowards, Memphis, Tennessee

Homemade Vegetable Soup

2   pounds stew meat
1   small onion, diced
1   small green bell pepper,
    diced
1   small clove garlic,
    crushed
3   15-ounce cans mixed
    vegetables
5   medium potatoes, cut
    up
1   15-ounce can okra
    Salt and pepper to taste
3   tablespoons sugar

In a large pot, cook the stew meat, onion, bell pepper, and garlic until the meat is almost brown. Add the mixed vegetables, potatoes, okra, and salt and pepper. Cook until the juice becomes thick. Add the sugar. Allow to simmer for about 2½ hours.

Makes 10 servings

Mary Jenkins, personal cook for Elvis Presley

Elvis' personal cook, Mary Jenkins

> *Never make small plans in life. Live boldly and remember that God forgives our faults, both great and small.*
> —Roland Bramblette

> *Be kind one to another, and love one another as He loves us. Stay close to the Lord, and have love in your hearts for people. Feel their hurts and share their joys.*
> —Eleanor Lustrea

Start Your Party Off with Welcome Dip!

1   8-ounce package cream cheese
1   12-ounce can corned beef
1   10¾-ounce can cream of
    mushroom soup
1   cup mayonnaise
    Green onions and/or celery, chopped
1   envelope Knox unflavored gelatin
¼   cup hot water

In a bowl, mix the cream cheese and corned beef together with a fork. Add the cream of mushroom soup and mayonnaise. Add green onions and/or celery (for flavor and color). Dissolve the unflavored gelatin in the hot water and add to the cream cheese mixture. Pour into a lightly-oiled mold. Refrigerate.

Makes 8 servings

Suzanne Whitney, New York, New York

Tantalizing Fruit Crush

3   cups water
2   cups sugar
1   46-ounce can
    pineapple juice
3   bananas
    Ginger ale

In a blender, combine the water, sugar, pineapple juice, and bananas, and blend until smooth. Pour into ice trays and freeze.

Fill a tall glass with the cubes and pour ginger ale over them. You will have an instant summer punch drink sure to tickle your innards!

Peggy Benson, Benson Publishing, Nashville, Tennessee, coauthor of Friends Through Thick and Thin

Cheese Ball

2   8-ounce packages
    cream cheese, softened
2   green onions, chopped
1   tablespoon seasoned
    salt
1   small package smoked
    ham, chipped
    Chopped nuts

In a medium bowl, mix the cream cheese with the onions, salt, and smoked ham. Mix thoroughly. Shape into a ball. Roll in chopped nuts. Refrigerate.

Makes 10 to 12 servings

Dimple Williams, Burnout, Alabama (Edie's childhood community)

Potato Chips

1½ pounds baking potatoes (4 medium), peeled *1 quart corn oil*	Using a vegetable slicer, slice the potatoes crosswise into very thin slices. In a bowl, soak in very cold water for 30 minutes; rinse. Repeat at least 3 more times to remove a good deal

of the starch. Pour the oil into a heavy 3-quart saucepan or deep-fryer, filling no more than one-third full. Heat over medium-high heat to 375°.

Meanwhile, drain the potatoes and dry thoroughly with towels. Place the potatoes, about 1 cup at a time, in the frying basket. Carefully lower into the oil; stir. Fry for 2 to 3 minutes or until golden brown. Drain on paper towels. If desired, sprinkle with salt.

Serve immediately; chips will not stay crisp if stored.

"Do Ahead" two-step method: Several hours in advance, fry the potato slices 1 minute or until tender, but not brown. Drain on paper towels. At serving time, reheat the oil to 375°. Place the blanched potatoes, about 1 cup at a time, in the frying basket. Fry 1 to 2 minutes or until golden. Drain on paper towels.

Serve immediately; chips will not stay crisp if stored.

Makes about 6 cups

Dimple Williams, Burnout, Alabama
(Edie's childhood community)

The Missing "Linc" in Fitness

- Visualize what you want to happen physically and mentally, and envision the "new you." This is the first step to getting in shape, both inside and out!
- Research different methods of working out and dieting.
- Take this research and apply it to your life by using the information to form a fitness plan that will help you achieve your goal.
- Follow your plan and remain positive. Do not give up, and, before long, your goal will become your reality!

—Linc Hand

Bill Gaither's Attitude for Life

Many people come in and out of our lives, but only a few make a difference by leaving an impression of love that lasts forever. Bill Gaither is one of those people.

He grew up in Indiana, and when he was in the sixth or seventh grade, he heard his first quartet on a 50,000-watt station in Indianapolis. It was a group called the Dixie Four. In those days, quartets would go to a big metropolitan area and get on a major station to do the broadcasting. The Dixie Four sang out of the old Stamps and Stamp-Baxter convention books. Bill had never heard those songs before, and he loved them. (They say that the music you fall in love with when you're in junior high is probably going to be the music of your life. That was true in his case.)

Bill begins his story by remembering his early years. He states, "I did not do any writing until I was in college. I was so impressed with the great writers, like Leroy Abernathy, Stewart Hamblin, and Mosie Lister, that I didn't think about trying to do what they were doing because they were so good. All the guys and I wanted to do was be able to sing like them. When I got out of high school, I sang professionally for one year. I eventually went back to school, majored in English, and taught school. While teaching, I met my wife, Gloria. She was a substitute French teacher. Getting a regular job was a good experience because it taught me responsibility. I had to earn a living, but during this time I also decided to start writing music.

Before too long, the songs that we were writing began catching on with the public. I then realized that I had entered the music profession. Soon, I

Gloria and Bill Gaither

family

started making recordings with my brother and Gloria. People wanted to hear more from us and they asked us to come to their community to sing." That was just the beginning of Bill Gaither's adventure into stardom.

He continues his story by saying, "I did not give up my day job of teaching just yet. My father grew up during the Depression, so the value of having more than one income was shown to me at an early age. Having another paying job really helped because I never had to worry about making ends meet the way other people did. In the beginning, we sent out tapes to prisons and nursing homes. Those folks grew up loving music, too, and sometimes music is the only thing that still speaks to them. They all know the lyrics and they know what is going on. Gloria and I also sent our music to Anderson University, a Christian university at home. Now we are on television. If someone had told Gloria and I that we would be on TV, we never would have believed them, but here we are. One thing that the years have taught me is to remain open to new ideas. My problem today is that there are too many new ideas with which I would like to become involved. So now I spend a great deal of my time learning how to prioritize my opportunities. In life, there is always a choice between something good and something bad—the really tough problem is choosing between something good and something even better.

"When it comes to the philosophies of life, I pick Philippians 2. It is one of the best guides that I know of. It reads of Jesus becoming a servant. He is our ultimate model. On my very best day, all that I am is a sinner saved by grace. As a child, I thought of holiness as a coat that you put on. I have found out over the years that, primarily, holiness is getting up every day. Holiness is your salvation, with fear and trembling, daily renewing your mind because we are human beings."

Bill Gaither's attitude is one of love for his fellow man. He is a true servant of God. There is no doubt that when this life is over for him, he will be remembered for his grace toward his fellow man, and he did it God's way. Another great book to read that shares the Gaithers' songs and stories is *Because He Lives* by Gloria Gaither.

faith

Easy Cheese Crispy

1   8-ounce package
     Cheddar cheese,
     softened
1   cup butter, softened
2   cups all-purpose flour
1   cup Rice Krispies (or as
     much is needed to help
     shape into rolls)

In a bowl, blend the butter and cheese and mix together with the Rice Krispies. Add the flour and roll into small bite-size balls. Press with a fork onto a lightly greased cookie sheet. Bake for 10 minutes at 350°.

Makes at least 80 bite-size cookies and it's great with chili!

Peggy Benson, Nashville, Tennessee

Marc's Easy Cream Cheese Rolls

1   8-ounce package of
     cream cheese, softened
1   4-ounce can mushroom
     pieces
1   10-ounce can of
     refrigerated crescent
     roll dough

In a small bowl, mix the cream cheese and mushroom pieces. Open the crescent roll dough and separate into 8 triangles. Spoon the cream cheese mixture onto the individual dough triangles and roll up. Bake at 350° for 10 to 13 minutes, according to the package directions.

You may want to make more than 8; they are very popular appetizers and finger food items at parties!

WARNING: Filling is HOT!

Makes 8 rolls

Edie Hand

Being a senior citizen is a wonderful thing! Seniors can make a positive change in the world by spending time with the less fortunate, helping the needy, and offering a smile and a helping hand. Above all, never give up searching for further ways to fulfill your life.

—Ruby Hostness

"Cracking up" with Lorianne Crook

Sweet & Sour Party Meatballs

1   *pound ground beef*

1   *pound hot sausage*

1   *cup milk*

1   *teaspoon salt*

1   *egg*

2   *slices bread*

1   *cup firmly packed brown sugar*

½   *cup vinegar*

½   *cup water*

1   *teaspoon cornstarch*

1   *tablespoon prepared mustard*

Mix the ground beef, sausage, milk, salt, egg, and bread well and shape into small balls. Place in a large casserole dish. Bake at 325° for 1 hour.

In a medium bowl combine the brown sugar, vinegar, water, cornstarch, and mustard. Mix well.

Remove the meatballs from the oven and pour the sauce over them. Return to the oven and bake, stirring frequently, for 45 more minutes.

Use as hors d'oeuvres or serve with vegetables.

Makes 8 servings

Reverend Frank and Ruth Munsey, Hammond, Indiana

Hot Onion Soufflé

12 to 16 ounces frozen
     chopped onions,
     squeezed and thawed
3   8-ounce packages
     cream cheese, softened
2   cups Parmesan cheese,
     grated
½   cup mayonnaise

Preheat the oven to 425°. In a bowl, combine all ingredients. Mix well. Spread in a shallow 2-quart casserole dish. Bake for 15 minutes or until done. Serve with large corn chips or melba toast.

Makes 10 to 12 servings

Mrs. Robert L. Potts (Irene), Florence, Alabama,
University of North Alabama

Gourmet

Hot Spinach-Artichoke Dip

1   10-ounce package
     frozen spinach (thawed,
     drained, and water
     squeezed out)
1   14-ounce can artichoke
     hearts, drained and cut
     into pieces
4   cups Monterey Jack
     cheese with jalapeño
     peppers, grated
1   cup mayonnaise
½   cup sour cream
½   cup Parmesan cheese,
     grated
1   teaspoon parsley flakes,
     chopped
⅛   teaspoon salt
⅛   teaspoon garlic powder
⅛   teaspoon white pepper
     Tortilla chips

In a large mixing bowl, combine all ingredients except the chips. Stir to blend well. Spread the mixture in a 2-quart glass baking dish. Bake at 350° oven for 15 minutes or until hot and bubbly. Serve with tortilla chips.

Makes 10 to 12 servings

Dianna Bender, Florence, Alabama

Holiday Christmas Goodies!

Happy Memories Mexican Dip

Cream cheese
Salsa
Grated cheese

Spread cream cheese in the bottom of a semi-flat dish (as big or small as you wish). Pour salsa (hot, medium, or mild) all over the cream cheese. Then sprinkle grated cheese on top (Cheddar or a mixture of all of your favorites). Microwave until the cheese melts and serve with corn/nacho chips.

You may add other layers, such as refried beans, olives, jalapeños, and tomatoes. Enjoy!

Misty Whisenhunt, Addison, Alabama

Shooting Star Seafood Dip

Cream cheese
Cocktail sauce
Crab meat or small
cocktail shrimp
Green onions
Crackers

Place softened cream cheese in a dish (you may shape it so it is round, if you desire). Pour cocktail sauce over the top. Add either crab meat or small cocktail shrimp on top of the sauce. Chop up green onions to top it off. Serve with crackers. Very festive!

Misty Whisenhunt, Addison, Alabama

I live each day allowing the Holy Spirit to lead me. It's very hard to remember sometimes that He is in charge, and I try to run ahead. When I do this, I often make mistakes, but if I take the time to listen, He will lead me in the right direction. I try to take some time each day for meditation because the quiet time allows me to listen to God. Too often, we spend so much time praying so hard that we don't take the time to listen to Him. When I meditate and listen, I find that the day flows and I remain centered and peaceful. If I don't I am simply scattered and miserable. I also take some time each day to do something good or helpful for someone else—even if it's just a phone call to let someone know that I am thinking about him or her or working on a civic project for the good of the entire community. I find these things very rewarding, fulfilling, and necessities in my recipe for life.

—Jean B. Williams, Jasper, Alabama

Carol Grace Anderson's Attitude for Life

*"It's important to grieve the loss of our loved ones
because we can only heal it after we feel it."*

∾

C arol Grace Anderson shares her philosophy above with great wisdom behind it. She is a speaker, an author of a book entitled *Get Fired Up Without Burning Out,* and the coordinator of special projects for the entertainer Roy Clark. She travels all over the country and speaks to corporations and associations, but the subject of her profession is not the only one she is an expert in. She is also an expert on dealing with grief, simply because she has struggled with the loss of her best friend, who was also her sister. Her strength and faith to deal with her loss were traits she picked up from her family.

Says Carol, "My dad has an active ministry in the South Bronx in New York City. He has had a ministry there since I was a little girl. When I was two, he had a gospel-television, live program every Sunday called *Life Lighthouse.* It had great music and variety, but it always had a message. There were trios and quartets and special music and sometimes I would sing. Both my parents are very musically inclined and I have been since I was little. My mom still teaches piano and travels around New Jersey making "house calls." My mother is eighty, my father eighty-three. My mother really witnesses to all of her students and their families. She teaches and ministers to them. She loves what she does and her students think of her as a saint. My father is still going into the Bronx and teaching kids things they would never have exposure to if he were not there. He plays the trombone and he sings."

Carol, along with her two sisters and her brother, grew up with these examples of faith, and Carol and her sister Marybeth let that carry over into their future careers.

"I had a band called Ladysmith and we used to play all over New York, New Jersey, and Pennsylvania. Someone heard my group and said we ought to go to Nashville and they set up an appointment at Chapel Music. Marybeth was in the band, too, and we went, played our demo, and got signed right away. We went back to New York and I finished out the year teaching. I had taught psychology in a jail for male heroin addicts for five years. I gave my notice and they told me my job would be waiting for me when I got tired of Nashville. I

friends

moved down there as a professional songwriter/background singer. My sister and I later became a duo, and Roy Clark called us looking for two singers. He hired us in 1980, and we toured with him until 1990. We were regulars on *Hee-Haw* whenever he sang, and we sang his back-up. It was a wonderful experience."

Carol and Marybeth would later travel with Roy Clark on the Friendship Tour that led them to faraway countries, including Russia. This was an unforgettable experience not only for the tour group, but for Carol and Marybeth, who increased the love in their own sisterly friendship.

Carol remembers, "Marybeth and I had such a wonderful time. It was an unforgettable trip. You don't ever forget it when you go to a place like Russia. At the beginning of the trip, we got on a train after we arrived at 11 P.M. in Moscow. The whole band boarded this train with a film crew to go to St. Petersburg. They put us in what was first class and everybody had a compartment for two. My sister and I had one and we scraped the ice from the windows and looked out at the midnight sky. All we could see was snow and chimneys with smoke coming out. The concerts were just as amazing. We could see the people with pain in their faces, but they would break out in smiles as Roy Clark sang. You could see the sadness in their faces, but their faces would light up when Roy hit the first chord. We always appreciated everything about every event we did together. Marybeth and I knew how to treasure every moment. That was our job, to travel and sing. We were sharing the gift of music. When people hear music, their faces brighten up. Marybeth and I strived to give our very best."

The efforts of Carol and her sister to give their best continued when they faced the beginning of a tough journey together.

Carol Grace Anderson, Roy Clark, and Carol's sister Marybeth, who died several years ago from breast cancer

friends

Carol says she will never forget it. "My sister was diagnosed with breast cancer in late 1993. She took it very well. She had taken a mammogram, but it did not show up because it was so small. She felt it, though, and followed up by going to her doctor. They did a biopsy and found that it was cancerous. So, she had a lumpectomy and they gave her three kinds of chemotherapy. I would go over there with her for her treatments and she had her cowboy boots on and her leather jacket. It was uncanny to see her looking like a star sitting in that chair. She had a faster-acting type of cancer, but went to MTSU anyway to finish up after her radiation. She had become an artist through this and she wanted to go into art therapy. Everything was fine until she went out for her morning walk one day and felt a pain in her hip. Then her back hurt so she went to a chiropractor. The chiropractor became concerned after a while had passed and her pain was still there. She went back to her regular doctor and then she called me. It was on March 7, 1995, and she asked me to go with her to have more X-rays. I will never forget that day because my dog, Cowgirl, had died seven days earlier from cancer and Marybeth and I had had our own ceremony for that. Here it was, just days later, and I was grieving a lot from that, when someone found a dog like Cowgirl. I brought her home that day, and that was when Marybeth called. I went with her for the tests and later the doctor came in and said the X-rays didn't look good. He said, 'I'm concerned.' I will never forget that. He did more tests the next day and that was the beginning of the last journey. God then gave her a lot of opportunities to have quality time with her family."

Carol says that Marybeth always had a zest for life. Even in her unfortunate death, she died with grace and hope.

"It was such a powerful experience to be there with her when she took her last breath. Her message is to live every moment and enjoy every moment while you're here. It was her time to go. She was blessed with so many talents and was one of the most loving individuals you could have ever met. She gave me so many messages and modeled such powerful behavior. She is still present and her spirit is still here. She didn't want things good, she wanted them great. Her passing changed my idea of death because there was power and beauty in it when she died. Everyone at the hospital said so. Her spirit was so powerful that we felt this strength when her spirit left her body, and it was amazing. We were uplifted and we had

friends

the ultimate peace in her death. We could feel her spirit in that room. We let her go. This was October 28, 1995. I feel that by Marybeth leaving, it gave me a new strength that I never knew I had because it was never tested in that way. I have the luxury of realizing that I am stronger than I thought because if I can make it through the loss of my best friend and sister, I can do anything. I decided I can give up or start up. So I started up and I began writing my book. It worked. What an example she was. I want to make it clear that many women have survived what Marybeth had. She should have beaten this, but she was one of the 5 or 10 percent that did not make it. It's important to grieve the loss of our loved ones because we can only heal it after we feel it. I know she's watching, but I cry when I need to but don't stay in the grieving."

Carol Anderson has picked herself up from the grieving process and moved forward with her life, all while hanging onto the powerful message that her sister left behind. Carol shares her experiences in her new book and is following in her sister's footsteps by being an example to others and changing the way people view the most precious gift of life.

Carol Grace Anderson, M.A., is a national speaker, author, and project consultant to Roy Clark. This former psychology teacher has been on the *Tonight Show,* appeared in a movie with Sandra Bullock, and wrote *Get Fired Up Without Burning Out!*

Laugh heartily
Love deeply
Learn constantly
Live fully
And believe strongly!

The above ingredients make for an enriched, fun life. Time flies by. Whatever we plan to do with our unique gifts and talents . . . NOW is the time to take action. Don't give up . . . keep fired up!
—Carol Anderson, lecturer, songwriter, and publicist for Roy Clark, Nashville, Tennessee

friends

Cranberry Percolator Punch

2   32-ounce bottles
     cranberry juice cocktail
4   6-ounce cans frozen
     lemonade concentrate,
     thawed and undiluted
6   cups apple cider
4   3-inch sticks cinnamon
2   teaspoons whole cloves
1   teaspoon whole allspice
2-3 cups light rum
     Lemon wedges (optional)
     Whole cloves (optional)

In a 30-cup percolator, combine the cranberry juice, lemonade concentrate, and apple cider. Place the spices in the percolator basket. Perk through the complete cycle of the electric percolator.

Remove the basket with the spices from the percolator, and stir in the rum. If desired, garnish with lemon wedges studded with whole cloves.

Makes about 20 cups

Jody Schefano, Dora, Alabama

We all have the ability to go to different places in our lives and, occasionally, we choose the option to listen to God to send us where we need to be. We must not be so grandiose that we believe that we change anyone's life, but rather to know that we plant seeds which grow at some unknown point in time. We must strive to do the right thing for ourselves and for others in our lives.

—Peggy Perdue, Freedom House
P.O. Box 20, Rogersville, Alabama 35652
(256) 247-1222

Freedom House is a home for chemically dependent women.
"In Honesty and Discipline There Is Freedom."

Wassail

1   gallon apple cider, divided
1   teaspoon ground cloves
1   teaspoon ground allspice
1   teaspoon grated nutmeg
1   teaspoon ground
     cinnamon
1   6-ounce can frozen
     lemonade concentrate,
     thawed and undiluted
1   6-ounce can frozen
     orange juice concentrate,
     thawed and undiluted
½   cup firmly packed brown
     sugar

In a large Dutch oven, combine 2 cups of apple cider and the spices. Bring to a boil. Reduce the heat and simmer for 10 minutes. Add the remaining apple cider, lemonade concentrate, orange juice concentrate, and brown sugar. Heat until very hot, but do not boil.

Makes 4½ quarts.

Jody Schefano, Dora, Alabama

Mint Dip with Fresh Fruit

1   cup whipping cream
¼   cup confectioners'
      sugar, sifted
1   tablespoon plus 1
      teaspoon green créme
      de menthe
1   large cantaloupe, cut
      into cubes
30 strawberries (1 to 2
      pints)
1   fresh pineapple, cut into
      30 bite-size pieces
1   strawberry fan
      (optional)

Beat whipping cream at medium speed with an electric mixer until soft peaks form. Beat in the confectioners' sugar, and then the créme de menthe. Transfer to a serving dish. Surround with fresh fruit and garnish with a strawberry fan.

Makes 8 servings

Jody Schefano, Dora, Alabama

> To keep life fresh, learn something new each day. Don't believe a word of that old saying, "An old dog can't learn new tricks." Of course they can!! (Now, don't you feel better?)
> —Marguerite Kelley

Pineapple-Cream Dressing

1   cup pineapple juice
2   egg yolks, beaten
      Juice of 1 lemon
½   cup sugar
1   tablespoon prepared
      mustard
      Dash of salt
1   cup whipping cream,
      whipped

In a small saucepan, combine all of the ingredients except the cream. Cook over low heat, stirring occasionally, about 30 minutes, until smooth and thickened. Cool. Fold in the whipped cream just before serving. Serve over fruit.

Makes 2¾ cups

Edie Hand

*in the kitchen with my gourmet chef—
neighbor Jody Schefano*

Deviled Eggs with Red Caviar

40	hard-boiled eggs
³/₄	cup mayonnaise
¹/₂	cup butter, melted
	Salt and pepper to taste
¹/₄	cup dill, finely chopped
7	ounces large salmon roe caviar
	Dill

Peel the eggs and cut in half, lengthwise. Place the yolks in a food processor and chop fine. Add the mayonnaise, butter, salt, pepper, and dill. Blend until smooth. Spoon the mixture into a pastry bag with a large star tip and fill each half egg. Cover and refrigerate for 3 hours.

To serve, top each half egg with a few grains of red caviar. Arrange on a bed of dill or in an old-fashioned deviled egg dish.

Makes 80

Jody Schefano, Dora, Alabama

Phyllo Triangles Filled with Feta and Spinach

1	16-ounce package phyllo pastry
¹/₃	cup olive oil
1	bunch scallions, chopped
2¹/₂	pounds fresh spinach, washed
1	bunch parsley
1	bunch dill
¹/₂	pound feta cheese, crumbled
3	eggs, slightly beaten
	Salt and pepper
1	cup butter

Thaw the phyllo dough overnight in the refrigerator.

In a large skillet, heat the oil and sauté the scallions until soft. Add the spinach and cook until wilted, stirring frequently. Place the mixture in a colander and press out the liquid into a saucepan. Boil down the liquid until it measures 2 tablespoons. In a large bowl, mix the spinach, spinach liquid, and remaining ingredients until well blended. Cool completely. Taste and add salt and pepper as desired.

To assemble, melt and cool 1 cup of butter. Place 1 sheet of phyllo on a flat surface. Brush with butter. Top with 2 more sheets, buttering each. Cut the sheets in half lengthwise. Then cut each half crosswise into 6 equal parts. Spoon a teaspoon of filling onto each strip and form a triangle by folding the right-hand corner to the opposite side, as you would a flag. Continue folding until the strip is used. Repeat the process until the filling is used.

Preheat the oven to 400°. Place the triangles on a buttered baking sheet. Brush with melted butter. Bake for 10 minutes until golden brown.

NOTE: Once you get the knack of working with paper-thin leaves of phyllo pastry, you will be able to make a hundred variations of this hors d'oeuvres.

Just keep life simple and it will be calmer.
—Fannie Flagg, author of Fried Green Tomatoes and Welcome to the World Baby Girl

Makes approximately 45 to 50 hors d'oeuvres

Jody Schefano, Dora, Alabama

Integrity . . .

Years ago, a television show called *This Is Your Life* was quite popular. Each show reviewed the life of someone famous. People from that person's past came to pay homage, often surprising the subject with their appearance. A standard prop used on the show was a book that told the story of the subject's life.

Imagine that you are the subject of this show. What would people from your past say about you? What accomplishments would be recorded in your book? More importantly, would your book be a proud account, or would it be filled with misdeeds, self deception, and missed opportunities? What will God say when he reads it?

It is not too late to change what's been going into those pages of your book, your life. While the past pages are already recorded for posterity, there are blank pages remaining in your future. Only you can decide what will go onto these blank pages. And while you are thinking about how to fill those pages, consider the number of pages remaining in your book. How many pages do you have left? Only God knows. You can hardly afford to waste one.

Shrimp Vinaigrette Wrapped in Snow Peas

1	bay leaf	3	tablespoons Dijon mustard
1	pound large shrimp (28 to 30), peeled and deveined	1	tablespoon shallots, chopped
15	to 20 snow peas	1	teaspoon ginger, finely minced
1	small, green cabbage	1	clove garlic, finely minced
	Vinaigrette:	1	tablespoon dill, chopped
½	cup olive oil		Pinch of sugar
3	tablespoons white wine vinegar		Salt and pepper to taste

Add 1 bay leaf to a large pot of boiling water. Add the shrimp. Cook, stirring constantly, for 2 to 3 minutes or until done, being sure not to overcook. Drain. Immerse in very cold water and drain again. Place in a glass bowl. In a covered jar, mix the vinaigrette ingredients. Shake well and pour over the shrimp. Cover and refrigerate for 1 to 2 days, tossing every 12 hours.

String the peas and blanch in boiling water for 30 seconds. Drain and immerse in iced water. Drain again. Split the pods lengthwise so you have 30 to 40 separate halves. Cut a thin slice off the bottom of the cabbage so it will stand upright. Wrap a pea pod around each shrimp and fasten by piercing with a natural wood toothpick. Then stick each shrimp into the cabbage. Serve cold or at room temperature.

Makes 28 to 30 shrimp

Jody Schefano, Dora, Alabama

My Zeta Tau Alpha sisters, University of North Alabama,
1973 (that's me, fourth from the left in the front row)

Throw a Prom Party!

1. Decorate the area with Christmas lights.
2. Put old album covers on the walls.
3. Fix dance cards or prom books as souvenirs.
4. Use tables and chairs for guest seating, and use party favors to decorate.
5. Prepare a feast fit for a prom king or queen, and make admission into the event a high school picture that is later displayed at the table at which you enjoy your feast.
6. Award door prizes for guests that have changed the least (or the most!) since the time of their picture.
7. The attire is old prom dresses and tuxedos, along with corsages and outdated hairstyles.
8. Use Burger King crowns to adorn the prom king and queen named at the party.
9. Play a lot of oldies music and dance the night away.
10. Take pictures of all the guests for admission into the next prom party and as a reminder of a party-filled night of fun!!!

—Jill Rogers

Clam Dip

1   3-ounce package of
    cream cheese, softened
1   can minced clams
1   tablespoon tomato
    paste
1   cup sour cream
    Few drops Tabasco
    sauce
    Few drops of
    Worcestershire sauce

In a bowl, mix the cream cheese with the remaining ingredients. Be careful not to add too much Tabasco or Worcestershire, as it will mask the flavor of the clams.

Serve with chips, crackers, or raw veggies.

Makes 6 to 8 servings

Edie Hand

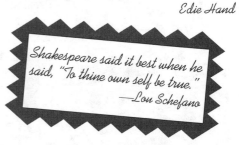

Shakespeare said it best when he said, "To thine own self be true."
—Lou Schefano

Cold Stuffed Mushrooms

3   ounces cream cheese,
    softened
2   ounces bleu cheese,
    crumbled
2   green onions, chopped
½   stalk chopped celery
16 large mushrooms

In a bowl, mix the cream cheese with all of the ingredients except the mushrooms. Cap the mushrooms by removing the stems. Fill the caps with the cheese mixture. Garnish with a paprika dusting or with finely chopped scallions.

Makes 16 mushrooms

Pamela Sue Repp, Nashville, Tennessee,
television producer, TNN

Mandarin Pinwheels

1   8-ounce package of
    cream cheese, softened
1   11-ounce can mandarin
    orange segments,
    drained and chopped
1   3½-ounce can chopped
    black olives
⅛   teaspoon paprika
¼   cup sliced green onions
6   ounces ham from the
    deli, thinly sliced
24 fresh spinach leaves
1   package 10 flour
    tortillas

In a small bowl, combine the mandarin orange segments, the softened cream cheese, and paprika. Arranged the flour tortillas on a flat surface. Spread each tortilla with the cream cheese mixture. Sprinkle half of the tortillas with onion and chopped olives. On top of that, layer fresh spinach leaves and thin slices of ham. Cover the ham layer with the tops (remaining tortillas with cream cheese mixture). Roll up each tortilla "sandwich" as it is finished.

Serve immediately or wrap in plastic wrap and refrigerate for at least 2 hours before serving. Unwrap, cut the rolls into pinwheels, and serve.

Makes at least 3 dozen appetizers

Edie Hand

Almond-Stuffed Dates with Bacon

1 pound pitted dates
1 4-ounce package
   blanched whole
   almonds
1¼ pounds sliced lean
   bacon

Stuff each date with one whole almond. Cut the bacon strips into thirds and wrap a piece around each date. Secure with wooden toothpicks. Place the dates on a foil-lined baking sheet. Bake at 400° for 12 to 15 minutes until bacon is crisp. Drain on a rack or paper towel. Serve warm.

Prepared dates can be frozen in advance and baked, unthawed, in a preheated 400° oven until crisp.

Makes 8 to 10 servings (60 hors d'oeuvres)

Jody Schefano, Dora, Alabama

Having fun doesn't always have to include others. In order to have a positive attitude in life, we must also learn to have fun by ourselves. To do this, we have to spoil ourselves sometimes—and that is the most fun of all!

Beginnings are scary and endings are sad, so enjoy the middle because it is truly the best.
—Angela Moore

Heart Healthy

Marinated Mushrooms

1 8-ounce package fresh mushrooms
1 medium clove garlic, minced
2 tablespoons green onion, finely chopped
2 tablespoons fresh basil, finely chopped
⅓ cup olive oil
2 teaspoons fresh jalapeño peppers, seeded and minced
⅓ cup fresh lemon juice
3 small strips lemon rind, yellow portion only
2 tablespoons dry white wine
¼ cup plain, low-fat yogurt

Wipe the mushrooms with a clean, damp cloth, and cut into quarters. Set aside.

In a shallow bowl, combine the remaining ingredients and mix well. Toss the mushrooms in the mixture to coat evenly. Cover and refrigerate, stirring occasionally, for several hours or overnight.

Remove the mushrooms from the marinade. Discard the marinade and serve the mushrooms cold.

Makes 8 servings of approximately 3 mushrooms each

a favorite of Edie Hand

Carol Grace's Lip-Smackin' Smoothie

1   pint low-fat vanilla
     frozen yogurt
1   banana
1/2 cup fresh pineapple
     pieces
1/2 cup fresh strawberries
1   cup orange juice
1   cup ginger ale
1   handful ice cubes

In a blender, combine all ingredients and blend until smooth. Serve in pretty glasses. Add a sprig of fresh mint if available. Delicious and nutritious all year long.

Makes about 6 servings

Carol Anderson, Nashville, Tennessee, lecturer, songwriter, and publicist for Roy Clark

Spinach Pinwheels

1   tablespoon margarine
1/2 cup onion, finely
     chopped
1   10-ounce package
     frozen, no-salt-added
     chopped spinach,
     defrosted
1/2 cup part-skim ricotta
     cheese
1   tablespoon fresh lemon
     juice
     Dash ground nutmeg
     Dash cayenne pepper
1   10-ounce package
     refrigerated pizza
     dough
1   egg white, slightly
     beaten
1   tablespoon sesame
     seeds

In a small non-stick skillet, heat the margarine over medium-high heat and sauté the onion until translucent. Remove from the heat.

In a small bowl, combine the onion, spinach, cheese, lemon juice, nutmeg, and cayenne. Blend well. Set aside.

Roll the dough into a 12" x 14" rectangle. Cut in half, forming two 7" x 12" rectangles. With a rubber spatula, spread half of the spinach mixture on each piece of dough. Roll up, starting from the long side. Pinch each end of rolled dough. Cover and refrigerate for 30 minutes.

Lightly spray a baking sheet with vegetable oil. Preheat the oven to 425°. With a sharp knife, cut each roll into 12 slices. Place the pieces on the prepared baking sheet. Brush each piece with egg white and sprinkle sesame seeds on each. Bake for 15 to 18 minutes.

Makes 24 pinwheels

a favorite of Edie Hand

You Can Do Hard Things

friendship

As a mother, I loved this story from my friend and colleague, Linda Long. She told me, and I want to share with you.

I often wonder how much of my well intentioned, but often unsolicited, advice stuck with my son during his "growing-up" years. Sometimes I had the strong suspicion my words were lost in the clouds, which is where I was sure his head was most of the time.

That's why you can image my surprise when, on a recent visit home, I learned just how much my repeated advice had meant to him, when I asked the question, "Son, what's the most important thing I ever told you?" Without hesitation, he answered, "You can do hard things. You always told me I could do hard things . . . and the older I got, the more I realized how right you were. Those words taught me to believe in myself. They stayed with me when I wanted to give up. In kindergarten, when I almost failed cutting and pasting . . . during that first football season when I had trouble even tackling the dummy . . . in college when I got my first stage managing job on a big production . . . then, after graduation, that first summer away from home—lonely, scared, and uncertain of my abilities—your words came back to me: "Son, you can do hard things."

During that same visit home, my grown-up child handed me a birthday card. The lines read, "To my mom, who taught me to dream and to learn and to try, with my feet on the ground and my sights on the sky!" It was signed "Your son, who is what he is thanks to you . . . you taught me I could do hard things."

Those are words that we can all live by. We all have reserves within ourselves that often go untapped and untried because we don't believe we can do hard things. You see, it's all in the ATTITUDE. Life is 10 percent what happens to us . . . and 90 percent how we react to it. If we believe it, we can do it. We can do hard things.

cancer survivor Tammie Allen with husband, Jeff

Simply Incredible Sisters

Incredible sisters from different walks of life.
Coming from the same place, having different outlooks on strife.

Making different decisions, having different
roads to walk.
Saying the same words, just a different way
to talk.

How different we were really, same Mom
and Dad,
Children are the priority, they keep us from
being sad.
Mothering is important, trying hard not to
be mad.

Business and career goals are always
being fed.
A man has always been there, dancing in
our head.

Circumstances change, a slap in the
face.
We have to prioritize, what a race.

The Lord must be at the top, we know this is true.
Family is important, all the family, not just a few.

A new life is mandatory, the choice has been made.
If only through the years our communication had stayed.

Many lessons we are learning, but this time not alone.
God placed us together in the beginning and now brought our hearts back home.

Caring, sharing, a reality that is true.
Our unconditional love is what we always knew.

Two sisters joining hands, example to set.
Teaching our loved ones, life's challenges can be met.

An inspired writing by Debby Reisner Rose, mother of six and sister of Darlene Real

Salads & Dressings

Brilliantly Bold Buttermilk Salad

1   large can crushed
     pineapple
1   large box strawberry
     jello
2   cups buttermilk
1   large container Cool
     Whip
½   cup chopped nuts

Heat pineapple. Add jello and stir until it disappears. Then add buttermilk, Cool Whip, and nuts. Stir and mix well. Pour into a mold and chill.

Mrs. Gerald Goode, Dora, Alabama

Vibrant Vegetable Salad

1   cup sugar
½   cup oil
1   teaspoon salt
¾   cup vinegar
½   teaspoon pepper
1   tablespoon bean juice

½   cup celery, chopped
1   green pepper
1   can tiny green peas
1   can french-style green beans
1   can white shoe peg corn
1   small jar pimentos
½   cup purple onion, chopped

Bring sugar, oil, salt, vinegar, pepper, and bean juice to a boil. Cool and pour over vegetables, adding peas last. Refrigerate overnight.

*Mary Tom Speer Reid, Nashville, Tennessee,
of the legendary Speer Family of gospel music*

Chilled Cranberry Salad

1   package fresh
     cranberries, chopped
1   cup sugar
2   small packages
     raspberry jello
2   cups hot water
1¾   cups cold water
3   apples, chopped, with
     peeling left on
     Juice of 2 oranges
     Nuts, if desired

Add together cranberries and sugar and let sit while preparing other ingredients. Mix together all other ingredients and add cranberry mixture. Congeal in refrigerator.

Charlotte Elkins, Jasper, Alabama

Brenda Russell's Attitude for Life

*Life is so open. You never know what's
going to come your way.*

∽

fun

The phrase above was never more true than when it took shape in singer and songwriter Brenda Russell's life. In fact, it is so true that it has transformed Brenda's entire way of looking at life. As a singer, Brenda has written and sang all of her biggest hits. As a songwriter, her work has also hit it big for the brightest recording stars in the business. However, Brenda did not always know what direction her life was going to take. Her ability to achieve her goals and aspirations is what adds the energy and inspiration to her life. She is not only one of the most talented women in the business, but she is also one of the most genuine and most fun.

Brenda says, "My attitude toward life is filled with inspiration. The most inspiring thing in my life is an awareness of God, and everything trickles out from there. God is my strength. I am a single mom and I divorced when my 22-year-old daughter was just 2. I think my career has been hard for my daughter because I have to put so much energy into what I do. However, I try to surround myself with positive people and, in order to do that, I have to become positive, too. I believe that like attracts like. If you want an element in your life, then you have to become that element yourself."

One of Brenda's most inspiring stories reflects on the time before she knew where her life would take her. It made a powerful impact on her and was the beginning of her most powerful impact in the music world. She remembers it well.

"The most inspiring story that I can share with others is when I was having the biggest struggles in my career. I was at a low point and it was scary. I was so frightened and I got down on my knees. I didn't have a record deal, but I had all this music inside of me and no way to utilize it. So, I got down on my knees and I said, 'O.K., God, not only do I want to get out of this hole I'm in, but I want to go around the world and sing and do all these things.' Within that year, I went all the way around the world and I had a hit record, because I released it to Him. I had Grammy nominations and my whole life turned around. I had a goal that only God could give me. When I let go, God brought a manager into my life, people to work with musically, and just a series of things. I just lifted my heart up because, you know, miracles are supposed to happen. Dave Koz and I met on that album, and I asked him to play on it. He was just starting out and now he is one of the most fantastic people I've ever known. I truly believe that we limit ourselves out of fear of failure and out of fear

fun

The fabulous Brenda Russell

of success. That's what keeps us from achieving our potential and our dreams. Carol King has been my idol and my inspiration. I looked at her and decided that's what I wanted to do. We wrote this wonderful song called 'Move the Moon' and it's going to be on this new album. It was awesome. I'm living my dream, but I want to keep growing at what I'm doing and fulfill my potential. If I can find myself as a whole person alone, then I am a much better partner. You have to find your own happiness and then you put out a much better energy to others. From my own experience, you must learn to trust your instincts. If you have something good to offer, get to it. Then weigh it with your inner voice that lets you know what you need to do. I write songs and all my material, and I'm an artist that does charcoal portraits. This experience is so uniquely different that there are no rules. You bring different people into your life, so you have to be awake enough to see that they can facilitate your dreams. Life is so open. You never know what's going to come your way."

Brenda Russell was definitely awake when she asked for her dream, and she is still awake as it manifests itself and comes true. She is a special artist in more ways than one. Right now she is painting a canvas of life that is paving the way for future stars looking for a break and a new attitude for life.

Keys to Family Sharing

1. Practice this with your extended family during an annual holiday celebration.
2. Have each person write out two thought-provoking questions, then collect them in a bowl or container.
3. At the close of a meal, bring the bowl to the table. Each individual draws a question, reads it aloud, and shares his or her answer.
4. Examples of some questions could be as follows:
   - "In your mind, what is a miracle?"
   - "What would you like to be doing ten years from now, where, and with whom?"
   - "If you could change anything in the past, what would you do differently?"
   - "What has been the highlight of your year so far?"
   - "What keeps you joyful and motivated, day after day?"

—Glenna Salsbury,
past national president
of the National
Speakers Association

family

Edie's aunt Clyneice Ledbetter and special friend Ben Speer having fun at a Gaither concert

Sensational Salad Dressing

¼   cup apple cider vinegar
1   cup cooking oil or olive
     oil
1   teaspoon mustard
½   cup sugar

In a blender, combine all of the ingredients and blend thoroughly until the sugar is dissolved and the mixture has thickened. Transfer to a container with an airtight lid and refrigerate until needed.

Serves 4 to 6

Chickie Bucco, New York, New York

Tomatoes with Tarragon Vinegar and Basil Salad

1¼ cups tarragon vinegar
1¼ cups water
½   teaspoon dried basil
1   teaspoon salt
2   teaspoons sugar
     Pinch pepper
4   tomatoes, peeled and
     sliced

In a small bowl, mix all of the ingredients except the tomatoes. Place the tomatoes in a flat, shallow pan. Pour the mixture over the tomatoes. Refrigerate for 30 minutes.

Serves 4 to 6

*Sue Hacker Hardesty, Highland, Indiana,
mother of Edie Hand*

Kathy's Killa Basilica

1   head bibb lettuce
2   large ripe tomatoes,
     sliced ¼-inch think
     Salt
1   medium bunch fresh
     basil
2   large fresh Mozzarella
     balls, sliced ¼-inch
     thick
     Extra virgin olive oil
     Ground pepper

Line a serving platter or 6 salad plates with lettuce. Arrange the tomato slices on the lettuce and sprinkle the tomatoes with salt. Place the basil leaves on the tomatoes and top with the sliced Mozzarella. Drizzle with olive oil and season with the freshly ground pepper.

Serves 6

*Tony Brown, Nashville, Tennessee,
president, MCA Records Nashville*

Hot Potato Salad

6   medium potatoes
2   tablespoons bacon
2   tablespoons all-purpose
    flour
1   cup water
3   tablespoons cider
    vinegar
    Salt and pepper to taste
1/3 cup chopped parsley

In a big saucepan, cook the potatoes in their jackets in a little water for about 20 minutes.

Drain. Peel and slice, and place the potatoes in a large bowl. Fry the bacon and remove from the pan. Let the bacon drain on a paper towel. Add the flour to the bacon drippings in the pan, mix, and cook for 1 minute. Gradually add the water and stir. Stir in the vinegar and the salt and pepper, then cook for 1 minute. Pour the sauce over the potatoes, and sprinkle with crumbled bacon and parsley.

Serves 6

Lela Hacker, Russellville, Alabama

Ronnie's Corn Salad

2   12-ounce cans Green
    Giant shoe peg corn,
    drained
1   box fresh cherry
    tomatoes, cut into
    quarters
1   green bell pepper,
    seeded and chopped
1   cucumber, peeled,
    seeded, and chopped
1/2 cup nonfat sour cream
1/4 cup mayonnaise
2   tablespoons white
    vinegar
1/2 teaspoon celery seed
1   teaspoon dry mustard
1   teaspoon black pepper
2   teaspoons salt

In a large, non-metallic bowl, mix all the vegetables together. In a separate bowl, combine the sour cream and the remaining ingredients. Pour over the vegetables and mix thoroughly. Cover and refrigerate overnight. Serve with barbecue or hamburgers, or stuffed in a tomato.

Serves about 6

Ronnie McDowell, Nashville, Tennessee,
singer/songwriter/sculptor
(as found in The Presley Family and Friends
Cookbook*)*

Ronnie McDowell shows off
the 1954 "Elvis Mobile"

Crab Salad

1   8-ounce package
     Alaskan king crab,
     thawed, or 1 7½-ounce
     can Alaskan king crab

1   pound fresh green
     beans

1   medium onion, thinly
     sliced

2   eggs, hard-cooked

1   cucumber, scored and
     sliced

1   tomato, cut into
     wedges
     Romaine lettuce
     Parsley

Oil and Vinegar Dressing:

½   cup olive oil

1¼   cups white wine
     vinegar

2   teaspoons parsley,
     chopped

½   teaspoon garlic salt
     Dash white pepper

Drain and slice the crab meat. Steam the green beans. Slice the onion, eggs, cucumbers, and tomato. Place the crab on the lettuce in the center of the platter. Arrange the remaining ingredients around the crab and garnish with parsley.

In a small bowl, combine the olive oil, white wine vinegar, parsley, garlic salt, and pepper. Mix well. Pour the oil and vinegar dressing over each serving.

Serves 4

Edie Hand

In all your ways, acknowledge God and He shall direct your paths. (Proverbs 3:6)
—Margie Rudolph

"*Be still and know that I am God . . .* " Psalm 46:30

I rejoice in each day and thank God for His will and plan for my life. I start and end each day in devotion, thankful for the opportunity to live life to the fullest, and, most of all, because my steps are ordered by the Lord.

—Dr. Trevy McDonald, Chicago, Illinois

Home-Made Children
(delicious, nutritious, and very healthy for all)

As I write this recipe there is bread "raising" on my hearth—and children "raising" in my home. The end product is not yet finished, but the ingredients have been carefully selected, measured, and blended, and the "Recipe Book" promises: "Train up a child in the way he should go, and when he is grown he will not depart from it." (Proverbs 22:6) Having followed the "Recipe Book," I trust the author!

Measure into home two parents in love and a few children (use own discretion on number; we prefer 3).

Add, stirring constantly, yeast (we recommend only one brand, Jesus Christ).

Stir in wisdom (as much as possible from God's word, previous training, and lots of common sense), truth (very important for consistent results), patience (ample portions needed throughout), kindness (large volumes), gentleness (soften before adding), discipline (with fairness, measured in a clean container), love (full measure, pressed down, shaken together, and even let it overflow the cup), and laughter (knead in as much as possible, let permeate throughout the whole batch). All ingredients should be measured out using a container of prayer (please do not substitute anything else for prayer).

For excellent eating and preserving quality, keep dough as soft and pliable as possible, but not sticky—just so you, with God's help, can handle it.

When mixed till smooth and elastic (about 18 years), round up in a greased bowl (symbolic of life's struggles) and cover with a damp cloth (we learn through failures as well as victories).

Let rise in a warm place (the environmental temperature for "raising" is very important) until double in size (about 4-8 years after high school).

Dough will be ready to be divided and made into all shapes of beautiful men and women to be used as "bread" (the Staff of Life) for other people's lives.

Guaranteed-Godly results!

—Naomi Rhode, author, lecturer, *More Beautiful than Diamonds*, *The Gift of Friendship*

faith

Corn Bread Salad

1   cup self-rising
    cornmeal
1   teaspoon all-purpose
    flour
½   cup (1 stick) margarine
2   eggs
1   8-ounce container sour
    cream

Topping:
1   cup onion, chopped
1   cup bell pepper,
    chopped
1   cup fresh tomato,
    chopped
1   cup small peas, drained
1   cup sweet pickles,
    cubed
1   cup mayonnaise
1   cup grated cheese
1   10-ounce bottle bacon
    bits

Preheat the oven to 400°. In a large bowl, mix the cornmeal, flour, margarine, eggs, and sour cream together. Spoon into a greased baking dish and bake for 20 to 25 minutes. When done, crumble the corn bread into the salad bowl.

In a medium bowl, mix the vegetables, mayonnaise, and cheese together. Spoon the vegetable topping over the crumbled corn bread. Sprinkle bacon bits over the top of the salad. Serve.

Serves 4 to 6

Edie Hand

Satisfying Frozen Fruit Salad

1   cup nuts, chopped
1   teaspoon maraschino
    cherries, chopped
1   9-ounce can crushed
    pineapple, well drained
½   pint sour cream
1   cup sugar
2   tablespoons lemon
    juice
⅓   teaspoon salt
3   or 4 bananas, diced

In a large bowl, combine all of the ingredients. Stir gently, but well. Spoon into 12 paper muffin tin liners. Freeze in the muffin tins. Remove the paper before serving. This is good served with turkey.

Makes 12

Francine and Cecil Blackwood, Germantown, Tennessee,
The Blackwood Brothers

Fantastic Fruit Salad Dressing

½   cup sour cream
½   teaspoon ground ginger
1¼ teaspoons ground
    nutmeg
⅛   teaspoon salt
1   teaspoon lemon juice
1   teaspoon sugar
    Quart of fresh fruit
    (your choice)

In a small bowl, mix the ingredients together well. Let stand for 10 minutes. Pour over a quart of fresh fruit—strawberries, blueberries, raspberries, or whatever else is in season.

Serves 4

Debbie Lustrea Paustch, Wheaton, Illinois

Raspberry Salad

2   bags mixed greens
1   pint fresh raspberries
    Feta cheese or
    Gorgonzola cheese
    Chopped walnuts
    Bottled raspberry
    vinegarette dressing

Mix greens, with raspberry dressing, in a large bowl. Toss lightly with crumbled feta or gorgonzola cheese and walnuts. Top with fresh drained raspberries.

Sue Dodge, Vienna, Virginia,
Southern gospel singer who appears on
Gaither Homecomings, TNN

The soul is the place where the heart rests.
—Doris Shaneyfelt

finance

The Ten P's of Financial Planning

1. **Personal Finance**—"If your outgo exceeds your income then it could lead to your downfall." Don't live above your income. Save a portion of everything you get and then you will be on your way to make your dreams come true. Step by step, inch by inch, it's a cinch.

2. **Protection**—Insurance is boring and not fun to think about. But in the event you have a bad car wreck or a tree falls on your home during a storm (or whatever the crisis), it pays to have an umbrella of coverage over you to protect you from loss. Unforeseen circumstances can ruin your plans for reaching your financial goals.

3. **Pay yourself first**—Read the book, *The Richest Man in Babylon.* Sometimes the simplest ideas are the best. If you get a dollar, save ten cents of it. Always put 10 percent aside for yourself. Then look at the magic of compounding interest. Calculate what a penny doubled everyday for thirty days would be—you will be amazed. That is the sure way to get rich, slowly.

4. **Purpose**—If you don't know where you are going, any road will get you there. Know where you want to go. Write down your goals. Think about them everyday.

5. **Plan**—Develop a plan to get you where you want to go. Like planning for a vacation, plan the route you will take, what vehicle will take you there, etc.

6. **Produce**—Make your days productive by producing income and put a portion of that aside for your future dreams.

7. **Proceed**—Proceed with caution and wisdom. Keep your ears open for the things that happen around you that will affect your goals. If you need to make adjustments in your plans to allow for new economic and investment changes, then do so. Don't hesitate.

8. **Preserve**—Preserve your financial future by living within your means and staying out of debt. Make the decisions

that will preserve your assets and don't give into the temptation to dip into your savings for extravagant pleasures.

9. **Persist**—Don't stop! Keep on keeping on no matter what. Even in hard times, when you are tempted to forego that savings this month, don't. Remember, you'll be glad that you did and your persistence will pay very handsome rewards down the road.

10. **Pray**—Pray for God's blessings and direction to be a good steward of your money. Do your part, and then ask God to bless your efforts. When you put your hand to doing something, He will reward you.

This may sound too simple. But the people who do the right things day in and day out, week after week, year after year, and never give up, will grow their nest egg and one day retire with a sense of satisfaction. The key is to JUST DO IT!

—*Brenda Lawson*

finance

Legacy

My legacy to you
Is the avid love
For books and reading.
This gift
Has been a rare gem
Entrusted
In my possession
For as long
As I can remember—
I bequeath to you
The golden key to knowledge,
Found tucked away
Between
The covers of books.
Reach out—
Accept this endowment—
Use it lavishly—
Its worth is greater than riches!

—*Doris Shaneyfelt, Jasper, Alabama*

Gourmet

Rouge et Noir Salad

2   bunches watercress
    (³/₄ to 1 pound total),
    washed and crisped

³/₄ pound mushrooms,
    sliced

1   3¹/₂-ounce can pitted
    ripe olives, drained

18 cherry tomatoes,
    halved

1   egg yolk

¹/₄ cup lemon juice

¹/₂ teaspoon each of sugar
    and dry basil

¹/₄ teaspoon each of salt
    and ground nutmeg

¹/₈ teaspoon white pepper

¹/₂ cup salad oil

Remove and discard coarse watercress stems (you should have about 1¹/₂ quarts). In a large bowl, combine watercress, mushrooms, olives, and tomatoes. Cover and refrigerate for at least 2 hours or up to 4 hours.

In a blender or food processor, combine egg yolk, lemon juice, sugar, basil, salt, nutmeg, and pepper; whirl until smooth. With motor running, slowly pour in oil and whirl until thickened. If made ahead, cover and refrigerate for at least 2 hours or up to 4 hours.

Arrange salad on individual plates and drizzle with dressing. Serve immediately.

Makes 6 servings

a favorite of Edie Hand
as found in Sunset Fresh Ways with Salads

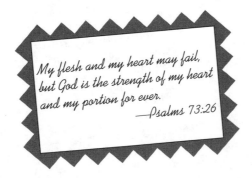

*My flesh and my heart may fail,
but God is the strength of my heart
and my portion for ever.*
—Psalms 73:26

Strawberry Chicken Salad Plates

Steeped chicken breasts
(recipe follows)

Fruit Vinegar Dressing
(recipe follows)

Butter lettuce leaves,
washed and crisped

2   cups strawberries,
    halved

2   kiwi fruit, peeled and
    sliced

Orange zest (optional)

Slivered green onion
tops (optional)

Orange slices (optional)

Prepare steeped chicken breasts and fruit vinegar dressing; set aside. (At this point, you may cover and refrigerate until next day.)

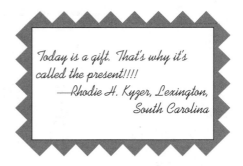

Today is a gift. That's why it's
called the present!!!!
—Rhodie H. Kyzer, Lexington,
South Carolina

Steeped Chicken Breasts:

Cut 2 small whole chicken breasts in half. In a wide 4 to 5 quart pan, bring 3 inches of water to a rolling boil over high heat. Quickly immerse chicken in water. Remove pan from heat, cover tightly, and let steep for 15 minutes; do not uncover until time is up. Chicken is done when meat in thickest portion is no longer pink when slashed. Drain chicken and place in ice water until cool; drain again. Remove and discard skin and bones; pat dry.

Fruit Vinegar Dressing:

1/2 cup salad oil

1/4 cup strawberry,
     raspberry, or cider
     vinegar

2   tablespoons sugar

1/2 teaspoon each of salt,
     paprika, and dry
     mustard

1   green onion, finely
     chopped

Combine all and mix until well blended.

Line individual plates with lettuce leaves. Cut each chicken breast crosswise into 1/2-inch thick slices. Reassemble each chicken breast in center of a plate, separating slices slightly. Arrange strawberries and kiwi slices beside chicken. Drizzle with some of the dressing, if desired. Garnish with orange zest, green onion tops, and orange slices, if desired. Pass remaining dressing at the table.

Makes 4 servings

a favorite of Edie Hand
as found in Sunset Fresh Ways with Salads

Grilled Salmon Salad

2	large bunches Romaine lettuce
1	red bell pepper
1	English cucumber
5	green onions
1	big red onion, separated into rings
2	teaspoons olive oil
2	tomatoes, chopped
4	8-ounce salmon fillets
	Juice of lemon and lime
	Cajun Seafood Magic
1	cup honey mustard dressing—get this in the dairy or produce section. We choose a refrigerated, low fat one.

Chop lettuce, bell pepper, cucumber, green onion, and red onion rings. Toss together. Put tomatoes on top.

Preheat grill to a medium heat. Wash salmon and pat dry with paper towel, then squeeze the juice of lemon and lime on the salmon fillet. Lightly brush each fillet with oil, then coat on both sides with Seafood Magic. Grill 3 minutes per side, or until it flakes easily. Cut fillets into bite size chunks.

Place salad greens on a large dinner plate and place grilled salmon chunks on top of salad greens. Drizzle honey mustard dressing over the top of salad and salmon. Grind fresh black pepper over the salad.

Serves 4

*Jessie Colter, Nashville, Tennessee,
singer and songwriter*

Jessie with her husband, Waylon Jennings

Rice & Cauliflower Salad

½ cup uncooked rice
    (steam and cool,
    Minute Rice is best)
1   small onion, chopped
10 stuffed olives (green-
    sliced)
¼   cup mayonnaise
    Juice of ½ lemon
1   8-ounce can shrimp
½   cup green pepper,
    chopped
1   cup cauliflower sections
    Dash of Tabasco
    Salt and pepper

Mix all ingredients together. I double, even triple, or make it as large as needed for the occasion. It is a wonderful dish for summer and goes well with bar-b-que or sandwiches.

Serves 4.

Jessie Colter, Nashville, Tennessee,
singer and songwriter

> *Character is a by-product; it is produced in the great manufacture of daily duty.*
> *—Woodrow Wilson*

Grilled Chicken Salad

6   boneless, skinless
    chicken breasts
2   tablespoons olive oil
    Cajun Seasoning
    Poultry Magic
2   bunches of Romaine
    lettuce
8   green onions, sliced
    thin
1   purple onion, sliced
    diagonally
1   cucumber, diced
2   tomatoes, diced
1   red bell pepper, cut
    1½ x ¼ matchsticks
2   boxes Uncle Ben's Long
    Grain and Wild Rice
    Original Recipe (5
    minute cooking recipe)
1   cup low fat honey
    mustard dressing

Baste chicken breasts in olive oil and sprinkle generously with Poultry Magic. Refrigerate for 2-8 hours.

Make the salad; discard outer leaves from the romaine and chop up or tear into bite-sized pieces. To this, add green onions, purple onions, cucumbers, tomatoes, and red bell pepper.

Grill the chicken until done and slice in thin long strips, approximate ¼-inches thick.

Cook the rice according to package directions, but omit the butter.

To assemble the salad, put the greens in a big circle on the plate leaving a little hole in the center. It should look like a donut or tire. In the center hold, place 1 cup of rice. Divide the chicken evenly and place on top of the salad greens. Spoon the honey mustard dressing over the entire salad and rice. Grind fresh pepper over the top and serve.

Serves 6

Jessie Colter, Nashville, Tennessee,
singer and songwriter

Lime-Flavored Gelatin Salad

1   package lime-flavored
     gelatin
1   cup hot water
1   cup miniature
     marshmallows
1   3-ounce package cream
     cheese
1   can crushed pineapple,
     undrained
½   cup nuts, chopped
½   pint whipping cream,
     whipped

Dissolve gelatin in hot water. Add marshmallows immediately. Breakup cream cheese in bits and add to gelatin mixture. Stir. Cool and add crushed pineapple; refrigerate until partially set. Stir in nuts. Fold in whipped cream. Pour in mold and chill.

Mary Whitney, Tulsa, Oklahoma

Ben Speer, Edie, Brenda, and Jim and Eileen Riley

Gorgeous Spring Salad

1   bag of Spring Green
     Baby Lettuces
4   scallions, cleaned and
     cut in ¼-inch pieces
1   avocado, peeled, pitted
     and cubed
1   can artichoke hearts,
     drained and cut in half
1   container cherry
     tomatoes, each tomato
     cut in half

Dressing:
¼   cup good Balsamic
     vinegar
½   cup extra-virgin olive
     oil
1   clove garlic, crushed

Wash greens in cold water and dry. Place in large bowl, and add other fresh ingredients. In a small jar, mix ingredients for dressing. Put top on jar and shake well to mix. Dressing may be made a day ahead so garlic will infuse flavor with oil & vinegar. Remove garlic before adding dressing to salad.

Add dressing to salad and toss well. Serve immediately.

Makes 4 large salads or 6 small salads

Ellen Riley, Birmingham, Alabama
assistant garden editor, Southern Living

Broccoli Salad

Water chestnuts
Romaine lettuce
3   boiled eggs
¼   cup olives
Broccoli flowerets
Parmesan cheese
Mayonnaise

Salt and pepper to taste—toss.
Enjoy!

Brenda Hill, Prattville, Alabama

Edie, Brenda, Linda, Wilma, Joanne, and Judy—Edie's monthly lunch bunch.

Spinach Salad

Dressing:
(Blend in blender until well blended and thickened. Store in refrigerator until ready to serve on salad.)
1   cup salad oil
¾   cup sugar
⅓   cup ketchup
¼   cup vinegar
1   medium onion, chopped
2   tablespoons Worcestershire sauce

Salad:
(Mix the following ingredients and chill in refrigerator until ready to serve with above dressing.)
1   bag of spinach that has been rinsed and drained (discard coarse stems before tearing spinach into bite-sized pieces for salad)
1   can bean sprouts, drained
1   can sliced water chestnuts, drained
3   hard boiled eggs, coarsely chopped
5   cooked strips of bacon, chopped

Marline Sellers, Florence, Alabama,
University of North Alabama alumnae and member of Zeta Tau Alpha Fraternity

A Little Tip on Child-Raising

Ingredients: 1 cup of Proverbs 22:6
                  2 tablespoons of Proverbs 19:18
                  A dash of Proverbs 23:13
                  A pinch of Ephesians 6:4
                  1 teaspoon of Proverbs 6:4
                  ½ cup of Titus 2:3-7

1. Mix all ingredients together.
2. Add a pound of persistence and an extra cup of love.
3. Whip to the right consistency and remember that this is recommended by our Creator!

—*Granny Ruby Hostness*

family

Anniversary Poem

For your "first anniversary"
Here is what I'd do:
I'd give you everything you'd need
In life to see you through.

Baskets filled with tactfulness,
Generosity will take you far.
I'd send you kindness more than you'll need,
Also a forgiving heart.

I'd send you honor, truth and right,
And bushels of compassion,
I'd send you dreams and loving thoughts,
And love beyond comparison.

I'd give you intuition and great vision,
Everywhere, for you to see.
I'd give you insight and deep concern,
And even E.S.P.

You'll need sharp instincts and listening skills,
Good attitudes and pure thoughts,
You must have foresight and common sense,
If only these could be bought!

You must have luck and patience,
For the crises in life are many.
I'd send you lots of four leaf clovers,
And a shiny, heads-up penny.

You'll need a sense of humor,
And adventure in your life,
Dealing with day-to-day concerns
Will be your biggest strife.

I'd wish for you much peace and joy,
And love where e'er you go,
I'd give you strength and wisdom
Like the prophets long ago.

All this, and more I'd give to you
Because you have all my love.
I pray to God, I pray each day
For special blessings from above.

Please, don't forget that wherever you go,
Please remember that whatever you do,
My wonderful, precious children,
I'll always love you.

—*Toni Drummond*

Heart Healthy

Greek Pasta Salad

1   12-ounce package tricolor rotini pasta

2/3   cup cucumber, unpeeled, seeded, and diced

1/2   cup green onions, thinly sliced

4   ounces feta cheese, crumbled

1 1/4   cups frozen no-salt-added baby peas, defrosted

1   cup red bell pepper, diced

1/4   cup light, reduced-calorie mayonnaise

1/2   cup low-fat cottage cheese

1/2   cup plain nonfat yogurt

1/4   cup green onion tops, thinly sliced

1   to 2 tablespoons fresh dill, finely chopped

1/4   teaspoon black pepper, freshly ground

Cook pasta in boiling water for 7 minutes. Remove from heat, drain, and place in a large bowl. Add cucumber, 1/2 cup green onions, feta cheese, peas, and bell pepper. Set aside.

In a blender or the work bowl of a food processor fitted with a metal blade, combine mayonnaise, cottage cheese, yogurt and 1/4 cup green onion tops. Process until completely smooth. Add dill and black pepper and process briefly. Pour over pasta mixture and stir to mix well. Cover and refrigerate until well chilled.

Serves 8 (1 cup per serving)

a favorite of Edie Hand
as found in American Heart Association Cookbook:
5th Edition

Let us be of good cheer, remembering that the misfortunes hardest to bear are those which never come.
—Amy Lowell, Coffee Time Thoughts

Carrot Raisin Salad

2　cups raw carrots, shredded

¼　cup seedless raisins

¼　cup light, reduced-calorie mayonnaise

¼　cup plain nonfat yogurt

2　tablespoons fresh lemon juice

In a bowl, combine carrots and raisins. Mix thoroughly. Set aside.

In a small bowl, combine mayonnaise, yogurt, and lemon juice. Stir to mix well. Pour over carrot-raisin mixture and mix well.

Serves 6

a favorite of Edie Hand
as found in American Heart Association Cookbook: 5th Edition

Edie

A gift sent from Heaven
To brighten the Earth
With soft words that
Soothe like warm breezes,
Carrying to others the
Depth of concern and love.
Never deserting or flitting
Into some unknown corner
Beyond the outstretched
Reaches of those in need,
A smile, an encouragement
Given freely from the
Very heart that survives
On love, hope, and trust.
Unknowingly leaving a path of
Footprints for others to follow—
The steps that lead up—never down—
Searching only for loftier heights!
A star out of its orbit
Glowing with light and direction,
Magnetizing the objects around
Forming one Heavenly body!

a cherished poem by Doris Shaneyfelt

4 Season's Blueberry Salad

Wash fresh blueberries and let drain. Measure 2 cups of blueberries into tight sealing container. Add 3 tablespoons of sugar or 2 packages of Sweet 'N Low with 1 tablespoon of water. Stir. Let set at room temperature for 1 hour. Stir again, then refrigerate. Blueberries are ready to eat or use in recipe in 24 hours.

To thicken fresh blueberries for salad recipe, put blueberries in small boiler along with 3 tablespoons of water and 1 tablespoon of cornstarch. Bring to a boil while stirring and then let cool completely before making salad.

2   cups blueberries with juice
1   8½-ounce can crushed pineapple with juice
2   3-ounce boxes of Black Cherry Jello
2   cups boiling water

Topping:
1   8-ounce package cream cheese
½   cup sugar
1   pint sour cream
½   teaspoon vanilla flavoring
½   cup pecans

Soften cream cheese and fold in sugar, sour cream, vanilla, and pecans. Spread over congealed salad. Top with pecans to decorate.

Serves 6

Joyce Knight, Sumiton, Alabama,
4 Seasons Garden Center co-owner

> Success is to be measured not so much by the position that one has reached in life as by the obstacles which he has overcome while trying to succeed.
> —Booker T. Washington

Appetizing Apple Corn Muffins

1   12-ounce box corn muffin mix
⅔   cup milk
1   egg
2   red or golden delicious apples, pared and shredded or finely chopped
2   tablespoons brown sugar

In a bowl, combine muffin mix, milk, and egg; mix just until dry ingredients are moistened. Stir in apples. Spoon batter into 12 greased muffin cups. Sprinkle with brown sugar. Bake in 425° oven for 15 to 20 minutes, until golden brown.

Makes 12 muffins

Mrs. Gerald Goode, Dora, Alabama

Do you feel like you're being pulled from all ways at once? There are times when I start the day out and run like crazy, just to end the day with exasperation because I didn't accomplish anything that I originally set out to do. The problem is that I have let the day control me, instead of me controlling the day. We should all have a plan for what we are going to do with our day. Whether you are a busy executive or a stay-at-home mom, you cannot accomplish anything if you don't control your time and efforts. So try planning your day's events right now and you will see the results sooner than you think!
    —I'm Edie Hand, and that's my attitude for life!

Racing legend Bobby Allison and family taking a break during the TNN taping.

Breads & Company

Boisterous Blender Banana Bread

⅔ cup Wesson oil
2   egg yolks
3   bananas, mashed
2   tablespoons buttermilk
1   cup pecans
1   tablespoon vanilla
1½ cups plain flour
1   teaspoon soda
1   teaspoon salt
1½ cups sugar
2   beaten egg whites

In blender, put first 6 ingredients; blend well. Pour into mixing bowl and add flour, soda, salt, and sugar. Mix well, then fold in beaten egg whites. Pour into greased loaf pan. Bake at 325° for 60 minutes.

Sidney Hicks, Jasper, Alabama

Edie enjoying lunch in Jacksonville, Florida, with nephews Terry and David

What makes humility so desirable is the marvelous thing it does to us—it creates in us a capacity for the closest possible intimacy with God.

—Monica Baldwin

Small Talk with a Twist

6   cups plain flour (not
     self-rising)

3   teaspoons yeast

1¼   cups milk

½   cup butter or
     margarine

1   cup sugar

2   teaspoons salt

2   eggs

1¼   cups pumpkin (sweet
     potatoes or winter
     squash)

2   teaspoons cinnamon

½   teaspoons nutmeg

¾   cup brown sugar

1½   teaspoons cinnamon

3   tablespoons butter,
     melted

½   cup chopped nuts

½   cup butter

1   cup brown sugar

1   tablespoon corn syrup

In large mixing bowl, combine 2 cups of flour and yeast. In saucepan, heat milk, sugar, butter or margarine, and salt just till warm and butter is almost melted, stirring constantly. Add to flour mixture; add eggs, pumpkin, cinnamon, and nutmeg, then beat at low speed for 1 minute, scraping bowl. Beat 3 minutes at high speed. Stir in remaining flour to make a stiff batter. Cover and refrigerate for at least 1 hour. (It can be refrigerated up to 3 days.)

In saucepan, combine ½ cup butter, 1 cup brown sugar, and the corn syrup. Bring to a rolling boil. Pour immediately into two 15" x 10" x 1" baking pans. Sprinkle with nuts. Set aside.

Divide chilled dough in half. Roll one-half into a 12" x 12" square; brush with 1½ tablespoons melted butter. Combine ¾ cup brown sugar and 1½ teaspoons cinnamon. Sprinkle the center third with approximately ¼ of the sugar-cinnamon mixture. Fold ⅓ of the dough over cinnamon-sugar center, and sprinkle approximately ¼ of the cinnamon-sugar mixture on the fold just made. Fold remaining third of dough over. (You now have 3 layers.)

Cut crosswise into 12, 1" stripes. Holding strip at both ends, twist in opposite directions; seal ends firmly. Place in prepared pans, about 1½ inches apart. Repeat with remaining dough. Cover; let rise in warm place till nearly double (about 1½ hours.) Preheat oven to 400°. Bake in 400° oven 18 to 20 minutes. Immediately invert pan; serve rolls warm. Store in covered pan, and microwave to re-heat later.

Makes 2 dozen

Sandy Mobley, Lynn, Alabama

Get in Shape Now!

1. **Set realistic goals.** Decide what you want to accomplish—weight loss, general fitness, or just improved performance. Set short-term attainable goals. After you reach those goals, set intermediate goals, and then finally set long-term realistic goals.

2. **Research.** Find out as much as you can about what it is that you want to do. Use a variety of sources, such as libraries, magazines, publications, or your friends.

3. **Develop a program from your research, and find a starting point.** Remember to start off reasonably with things that can be accomplished easily. If you do otherwise you will set yourself up for disappointment and failure when your goals are not met.

4. **Consult a physician.** Always start off with a solid foundation. Knowing where you *are* will help you get to where you *are going*. Getting a medical opinion makes good sense and will help you realize your limitations. This will also prevent needless injuries.

5. **Use the right equipment.** Training gear and equipment is a must. Make sure that you are outfitted with the proper gear. This will increase your enjoyment and appreciation, while at the same time reducing your chance of injury. Shop around, because it is not a good idea to spend great amounts of money until your commitment and interest grows. This will come as you reach your goals.

—*Willie J. Smith III, Birmingham, Alabama*
3-time gold medal winner of
Track and Field

fitness

Sassy Skillet Corn Bread

2   cups self-rising corn
     meal
¼   cup flour
2   teaspoons baking
     powder
2   teaspoons sugar
2   teaspoons salt
2   tablespoons
     mayonnaise
2   large eggs
1½   cups buttermilk

Mix all ingredients well (adjust butter as needed to make mixture very pourable). Pour into a large greased and preheated iron skillet (I use about 1½ tablespoons bacon drippings, but you can use cooking oil). You can use muffin tins, etc. Preheat and bake at 450° on top rack of oven. Cook until brown.

Linda H. LeDuke, Guin, Alabama

Edie hosting a MDA telethon.

Grandmother's Buttermilk Biscuits with Chocolate Gravy

2   cups self-rising flour
1½   teaspoons baking
     powder
¼   teaspoon baking soda
1   teaspoon sugar
½   cup shortening
1   cup buttermilk

Chocolate Gravy:
2   tablespoons cocoa
1½   cups sugar
2   tablespoons all-purpose
     flour
1   teaspoon vanilla
     extract
3   cups water

Preheat the oven to 450°. In a large bowl, combine the flour, baking powder, soda, and sugar. Cut in the shortening with a pastry blender or two knives. Add the buttermilk and knead until smooth and pliable. Roll the dough out on a floured surface to the desired thickness, or about ½ inch. Cut with a biscuit cutter and place in a baking pan. Bake for about 12 minutes or until brown on top.

In a saucepan, combine the cocoa, sugar, flour, vanilla, and water, and cook over medium heat until it boils. The mixture will slowly thicken. Cook for about 10 minutes. Pour over buttered hot biscuits.

Serves 10

This is my Grandmother Hacker's recipe. She raised her 12 children on these delicious biscuits for breakfast.

—Edie Hand

Landy's Banana Bread

1	cup sugar
1	stick butter or margarine
2	eggs
2	cups all-purpose flour, sifted
1	teaspoon soda
3	medium bananas, mashed
½	cup pecans, chopped
1	tablespoon water

Cream sugar and butter in bowl. Beat eggs and add to mixture. Blend well. Add flour and soda, then add bananas. Mix thoroughly. Add nuts and water. Pour into greased pan. Bake at 350° for 1 hour or until golden brown.

You can double the recipe and make a loaf for a friend!

Judy Hester Bodie, Mobile, Alabama

Southern Corn Bread

1	cup self-rising flour
1	cup yellow cornmeal
½	teaspoon salt
3	teaspoons baking powder
1	tablespoon sugar
1	cup milk
1	egg
2	tablespoons bacon drippings

Preheat the oven to 375°. In a large bowl, mix together the flour, cornmeal, salt, baking powder, and sugar. In a separate bowl, beat the egg. Add the eggs to the milk. Combine the 2 mixtures and stir well. In an 8" square baking pan, melt the bacon drippings. Add the melted drippings to the batter and stir. Pour the mixture into the baking pan and bake for 20 minutes.

Serves about 10

Sue Hacker Hardesty, Highland, Indiana
mother of Edie Hand

Cracklin' Corn Bread

1	cup self-rising cornmeal
1	cup buttermilk
1	cup pork cracklin's
½	cup self-rising flour
½	cup vegetable oil

Preheat the oven to 450°. In a large mixing bowl, combine the cornmeal, buttermilk, cracklin's, flour, and ¼ cup of oil. In an 8" skillet, heat 4 tablespoons of oil until it is very hot. Pour the batter into the skillet. Bake for 20 minutes or until golden brown, slice, and serve warm. Add a glass of hot tea and sliced onions and get set for the best 10 minutes of eating you'll do in the South!

Serves 8 to 10

Edie Hand

Johnny Minick's Attitude for Life

*"We are troubled on every hand yet not distressed,
perplexed but not despaired, persecuted but not
forsaken, cast down but not destroyed."
(2 Corinthians, chapter 4)*

❧

Many people believe that if only they were famous all of their problems would go away. They think that fame and fortune is the key to happiness and if they possessed that, they would be the richest people around. Those that have been in the spotlight, however, may disagree. Singer, musical arranger, and pastor Johnny Minick is one of those people. His attitude for life can be summed up by the verses above. He says that it is not always easy in life, but the word of God is his encouragement. Johnny has witnessed, firsthand, the downside to fame and fortune. He has learned through the experiences of others just how unhappy a person can be when he or she tries to fill the void in his or her life with worldly things.

Johnny is a member of the Happy Goodmans gospel group and he travels and performs with them. On one occasion, Rick Goodman (another member of the group) met Wayne Newton, and that experience had a great impact on Johnny's life. He remembers, "Rick had met Wayne and in their meeting they had talked about Wayne doing a country album. He was presented with the notion to come to Nashville and use a small band to create music in the studio. It intrigued him to think that you could do spontaneous arrangements like that and so he came to Nashville and we did the first session and developed a friendship. Rick got me involved because I was an arranger and producer. After that session, Wayne said he had recently purchased a letter that Elvis had written the last time he played the Las Vegas Hilton. Elvis had written the letter and thrown it away, and a maid had found it. Somehow it ended up in Wayne's hands and it had been authenticated as something Elvis had written. He brought it and Rick and I were looking at the lyrics because before I begin to look at something musically, I look at the lyrics. Immediately after reading the letter I saw in it a man reaching out to God in a big way. It reminded me of Solomon (in the Bible) who said, 'I've done everything,

friends

I've tried everything, I have everything, and it's all vanity.'
Elvis was saying that everything was at his fingertips. When it
boils down to the bottom line, Elvis realized that unless you
have a relationship with God, you really don't have anything."
The "bottom line" was something that Johnny, fortunately,
realized at a very early age. In fact, he says that God is the very
basis for his happiness, and not the fame and fortune that so
many seek to fill the void. "In just a few lines, I can sum up my
attitude on life by saying that I enjoy it tremendously because
I do what I enjoy doing and that's working for God with every
talent and ability that He has given me. So it's very easy for me
to find my center because it's all about God. I sing gospel
music and sing with people I love and I'm in the full-time ministry with the church and pastorate, not to mention that I'm
training other pastors. My church is located in Smyrna,
Tennessee, and I consider it transdenominational, although
it's an Assembly of God church, because I feel that doctrine is
important but denomination is not a prerequisite to having a
relationship with God. God is what will get you into heaven,
not your denomination. The relationship with God is what
brings salvation into your life."

friends

Johnny Minick of the Happy Goodmans

friends

Johnny began playing guitar when he was three and could accompany himself by the time he was four. He then began singing in church, went from guitar to piano when he was six, and then he got into the studio when he was seven. In the early 1970s, he developed a quartet and they became quite popular in the Little Rock, Arkansas, area. Before long, a gospel music promoter in the area that worked with the Happy Goodmans hired him. This was a break Johnny was looking for because he greatly admired the Happy Goodmans. He said, "Rusty Goodman took me aside and told me that one day I would play for the Happy Goodmans. I admired them and they had been one of the great influences in my life. I was called to preach when I was eleven years old and so I was very sensitive to the anointing of the spirit. When I listened to the Happy Goodmans, I felt that anointing of the Holy Spirit in them, so they were spiritual heroes for me. I had no desire to play with any other group but them and I was honored to be asked to work for them."

That was the beginning of what would lead to more life-changing experiences for Johnny, such as reading the Elvis letter with Rick Goodman and Wayne Newton. Not long after the letter was read to Johnny, Wayne asked him and Rick to come to Atlantic City and record it. It proved to be a success, landing several number one spots. Reflecting on the song and the letter, Johnny says, "All these things we call tangible are so temporary and as soon as the newness wears off, they have no value in them. That's why a relationship with God is so important. It lasts. From traveling with the Goodmans, they have made a big impact on my life. I traveled with them until 1977, when I began evangelizing. They called me if they did anything special and we became a family. I learned a lot about tenacity form Vestal. One of my themes is found in a song that Vestal sings called 'How Long.' The last line emphasizes what I've learned from Vestal and my parents. It says, 'I'm gonna make it, no matter how long.' It's what God can do and He never once has failed."

Johnny knows what it takes to make it in life—a personal relationship with God. He quotes the verse in 2 Corinthians, chapter 4 as his attitude for life, and he lives by it. And that is why he is continuing to excel in life . . . a man who walks and sings his talk, no matter how long the journey is.

Poppy Seed Biscuits

1   8-ounce package
    refrigerator biscuits
3   tablespoons butter,
    melted
    Poppy seeds

Preheat the over the 400°. Cut the biscuits in half; dip in melted butter. Place 3 halves, cut side down, around the edge of each muffin cup. Place one additional half in the center. Sprinkle with poppy seeds and bake for about 12 to 15 minutes or until golden brown.

Serve with additional butter.

Makes 6

Edie Hand

Spoon Bread

1   cup stone ground
     yellow cornmeal
2   tablespoons shortening
3   13-ounce cans
     evaporated milk
4   eggs, beaten
1½   teaspoons salt
1   tablespoon baking
     powder

Preheat the oven to 450°. In a large saucepan, boil the cornmeal, shortening, and 2 cans of the evaporated milk over medium heat, stirring constantly. Remove the pan from the heat and add the eggs, remaining can of evaporated milk, and salt. Quickly stir in the baking powder and pour into a greased 2-quart baking dish. Bake for 30 minutes.

Serves 8 to 10

Linda Sue Hacker Whitaker, Russellville, Alabama

A Good Morning with Coffee Cake

1   cup (2 sticks) butter
2   cups sugar
2   eggs
2   cups all purpose flour
¼   teaspoon salt
1   teaspoon baking
     powder
1   8-ounce carton sour
     cream
½   teaspoon vanilla
     extract

Topping:

½   teaspoon ground
     cinnamon
1   cup pecans, chopped
2   tablespoons sugar

Preheat the oven to 350°. Cream the butter, sugar, and eggs. Sift the flour, salt, and baking powder. Add to the butter mixture. Add the sour cream and vanilla. Beat for 4 to 5 minutes. Pour half of the batter into a greased and floured bundt pan.

In a small bowl, combine the cinnamon, pecans, and sugar, and sprinkle half of the topping on top of the batter. Spread the remaining batter on top, and then the remaining topping. Bake for 45 minutes.

Serves 10

Terry Blackwood, Nashville, Tennessee,
Famous Imperials/Gaither Homecoming videos

Zucchini Bread

2½ cups all purpose flour (all white or   3   teaspoons ground cinnamon
     half white and half whole wheat)   ½ teaspoon ground nutmeg
¼   cup powdered milk   1   cup oil
½   cup wheat germ   3   eggs, beaten
2   teaspoons baking soda   3   teaspoons vanilla extract
½   teaspoon baking powder   1   cup nuts, chopped
1   cup sugar   2   cups zucchini, peeled and grated
1   cup firmly-packed brown sugar

Preheat the oven to 350°. In a large mixing bowl, combine all of the ingredients.
Pour the batter into 2 well greased loaf pans. Bake for 1 hour.

Makes 2 loaves

Edie Hand

Light Rolls

1   cup milk
½   cup shortening
¼   cup sugar
1   teaspoon salt
1   package yeast
¼   cup water
4   cups flour
2   eggs

Heat milk, shortening, sugar, and salt until shortening melts, then cool slightly. Dissolve yeast in water.

When milk mixture is lukewarm, add yeast, 2 cups flour, and eggs. Beat well. Add one cup flour. Beat well. Remove beater and stir in ¾ cup flour. Let rise until doubled. Then punch down, and use remainder of flour for kneading. Make into rolls, and let rise about 1 hour. Bake at 400° for 10 to 12 minutes.

Candy Hemphill-Christmas,
Goodlettsville, Tennessee,
Southern gospel singer

A wonderful singer and
friend Candy Christmas

Peppy Peanut Butter Bread

1¾ cups sifted all purpose
      flour
2   teaspoons baking
      powder
¼   teaspoon baking soda
½   teaspoon salt
⅓   cup shortening
¾   cup peanut butter
⅔   cup sugar
2   eggs, slightly beaten
1   cup ripe bananas,
      mashed

Preheat the oven to 350°. In a medium bowl, sift the dry ingredients together. In a large bowl, cream the shortening and peanut butter. Add the sugar gradually. Add the dry ingredients and mix until light and fluffy. Add the eggs and beat well. Stir in the dry ingredients alternately with bananas. Do not beat. Spoon into a greased 5" x 9" loaf pan. Bake for 50 to 60 minutes.

Makes 1 loaf

Edie Hand

Fly-off-the-Plate Pancakes

Sister Schubert's *Secret Bread Recipes* is a must have for any kitchen!

Sister Schubert has shared this recipe of Fly-off-the-Plate Pancakes to reveal her authority on great baking. Enjoy her southern traditional recipe for pancakes.

1   cup all-purpose flour
1   tablespoon baking powder
1   tablespoon sugar
¼   teaspoon salt
1   large egg, lightly beaten

1   cup milk
2½   tablespoon sour cream
2   tablespoons butter, melted
      Vegetable oil

Combine first 4 (dry) ingredients in a large bowl. Combine egg and next 3 ingredients in another bowl, stirring with a wire whisk until frothy; add to dry ingredients, stirring just until smooth.

Heat a large griddle or skillet to medium-high, 375°. Lightly grease cooking surface with oil or coat with vegetable cooking spray. For each pancake, pour ¼ cup batter onto hot surface. Cook pancakes until tops are covered with bubbles and edges look cooked; turn and cook other side. Serve warm with butter and syrup or honey, if desired. Makes about 1 dozen.

The cooking surface for pancakes should not be greasy. Apply a little oil between batches and lightly wipe it off with a paper towel—or lightly coat the cooking surface with vegetable cooking spray between batches.

Sister Schubert, Troy, Alabama,
author of Secret Bread Recipes

Unbelievably Delicious Buttermilk Bread

2 teaspoons active dry yeast	1¼ cups cold buttermilk
½ cup warm water	5½ cups whole wheat flour
¾ cup very hot water	2 to 4 tablespoons butter
¼ cup honey	

Dissolve the yeast in the warm water.

Mix the hot water with the honey, and add the buttermilk. The temperature should be slightly warm.

Stir the flour and salt together, making a well in the center. Pour the yeast and buttermilk mixture into the well, and stir from the center outwards, incorporating all the flour. Test the dough to see whether more flour or water is needed and adjust accordingly. The bread is lightest if dough is slightly soft. For rolls, it should be quite soft. Knead about 20 minutes, adding the butter in cold bits at the end of the kneading time.

Form the dough into a ball and place it, smooth side up, in the bowl. Cover and keep in a warm, draft-free place. After about an 1½ hours, gently poke the center of the dough about ½-inch deep with your wet finger. If the hole doesn't fill in at all or if the dough sighs, it is ready for the next step. Press flat, form into a smooth round, and let the dough rise once more as before. The second rising will take about half as much time as the first.

Press the dough flat and divide into two. Round it and let it rest until relaxed, then deflate and shape into loaves or rolls. The recipe makes two loaves for 8" x 4" pans. Or shape the dough into rounds, flattening them slightly, and place in pie tins. Bake a little less time then loaves. These rounds, cut into wedges, make really good dinner bread. For rolls, one loaf's worth of dough make 9 large to 15 smaller dinner rolls in 8" x 8" or 9" x 13" pans, respectively. Sesame seeds complement the flavor perfectly, though they are not at all required.

Place dough in greased pans and let rise in a warm place until the dough slowly returns a gentle fingerprint. This dough makes a very high loaf when properly kneaded, so be a little bold about giving it time. Bake the bread in a preheated 325° oven for nearly an hour. Rolls take 15 to 20 minutes, depending on their size, at 400°. Brush the rolls with butter when they come out of the oven (the bread, too, if you feel fancy.)

Candy Hemphill-Christmas, Goodlettsville, Tennessee,
Southern gospel singer

Vestal's Spoon Biscuits & Cream Gravy

1	cup buttermilk	1³/₄	cups self rising flour
¹/₃	cup oil	1	large iron skillet

Mix all ingredients in mixing bowl until well blended. Spoon biscuit-size portions into well greased skillet. Place in hot oven quickly—do not allow to rise. Cook for 15 to 20 minutes in hot oven or until as brown as you like them.

Gravy:

¹/₂	pound roll sausage	3	cups milk
¹/₃	cup oil	¹/₂	teaspoon black pepper
3	heaping tablespoons self rising flour	¹/₂	teaspoon salt

Fry sausage in oil and pinch into small pieces. Remove sausage, add flour, salt, and pepper. Stir well and cook until medium brown. Add milk, stirring continually. If needed, add more milk until you get the consistency that you like. Add sausage and serve. Spoon over spoon biscuits.

Vestal Goodman, Nashville, Tennessee,
"Queen of Gospel music" and
author of Vestal! "Lord, I Wouldn't Take Nothing for My Journey Now"

Martin Luther King Jr. said that our lives begin to end the day we become silent about the things that matter. It is important to take note of the things that are happening around us. When something occurs that is a concern to us, we need to speak out and do something about it. If we do not speak up, our views become lost, and we become doomed to be silent in a world disappointed with the things that also matter to us.

—I'm Edie Hand, and that's my attitude for life!

Sister Schubert's Attitude for Life

Live life to the fullest in every moment.

∾

Patricia "Sister Schubert" Barnes has been cooking since she was a little girl. She never imagined that her philosophy above would transform into the pattern of life that has led her to become a fabulous success in the baking industry. Sister Schubert is not just successful because she is a wonderful cook. She is successful because she has carried the recipes and attitudes that her relatives shared with her through five generations, and they are still going strong. The amazing thing is that it all began with a bake sale and a station wagon in Troy, Alabama.

She begins, "I learned to cook from my mother, my grandmother, my great grandmother, and my mammy that raised me. I grew up in Troy, which is in the southeastern part of Alabama. It all started at my church then, St. Mark's Episcopal Church. The ladies at my church had a frozen food fair every year, and in 1989, the ladies asked me if I would let them put my rolls on their list and let people place orders for them. I said, 'sure,' and they had orders for over three hundred pans of rolls by the second year that they were taking orders.

Sister Schubert and her mother, Charlotte Wood, who is a breast-cancer survivor

I decided that if people in little Troy, Alabama, liked my rolls that much, then maybe other people would too! I had seen that we could manufacture the rolls in larger quantities, so I decided to give it a try and see if I could do it. Honestly, I believe that part of the reason for my success was that I truly just believed in what I was doing so much that I wouldn't let anybody discourage me. I didn't take no for an answer. I had a bargain with the Lord that if He would help me with this roll business, then I would help Him feed all the hungry people that I could. So our charitable causes are associated with organizations that help to feed the hungry and help benefit those that are victims of disasters."

When Sister Schubert decided to begin her business, she did not have the funding. That's where her "financial expertise" had to come in handy.

"I remember going down and applying for my first loan. My old station wagon was all I had for collateral, other than myself. But, the banker believed in me and he loved my rolls, so he took my title to my car and loaned me $25,000. I bought some used bakery equipment and started on a shoestring. Five ladies helped me in the beginning and then in four months, I was up to 50 employees. We got into Winn Dixie here right off the bat—within six weeks we were in Winn Dixie, and six weeks later, the Bruno's chain in Alabama contacted us and wanted to know why we hadn't presented the rolls to them. I told them it was because I couldn't make them fast enough! It was like a Cinderella story in the grocery business."

Sister Schubert's great fortune in her business has partly contributed to her positive attitude.

She said, "My philosophy of life is to live life to the fullest every moment. I get up in the morning every day and I say, 'Dear Lord, let me live this day the very best that I can.' I always try to have the most positive attitude possible rather than a negative one. One person said that the best way to describe me is as a person with lots of enthusiasm. That's my philosophy of life—to approach things in an enthusiastic way, in everything I do. Not only that, but God is my partner in this business and in my life. Everything I do everyday is geared around the verse that says, 'Let the words of my mouth and the meditation of my heart be acceptable in your sight, Lord.' He's been my strength."

finance

finance

Sister Schubert's success as a wonderful cook has spread into a cookbook entitled Sister Schubert's *Secret Bread Recipes*. It was published by Oxmoor House, and Sister remembers how they found her.

"Oxmoor house found me because of an article that *Southern Living* printed in 1992. When the writer from *Southern Living* first called and told me that she was with *Southern Living* and wanted to do an article on me, I said, 'Well, it's wonderful to talk to you. I'm Betty Crocker!' I thought somebody had been put up to calling me and telling me they were with *Southern Living*. She laughed and said, 'No, no, really I am!' Then it dawned on me that maybe she was serious. It was fantastic, and from that evolved the cookbook."

She may have had a small financial beginning, but Sister Schubert is now creating a financial bang.

"Nineteen ninety-two was my first half of a year in business and 1993 was my first full year. I had four items. I had my Parker House rolls, cinnamon rolls, orange rolls, and sausage rolls, and that was my line of products. I think my gross sales for that year were $140,000. This past year, we exceeded $12 million in sales. I have 200 employees, men and women. We don't discriminate and we're like a family. My family at home is wonderful, too. I have a wonderful husband, three daughters, ages 24, 20, and 10, and a 2-year-old son."

Along with enthusiasm, compassion is also her attitude, as is demonstrated with her charity work. One of the contributing factors to her compassion is her mother, who is a survivor of breast cancer.

She said, "My mother, Charlotte, was 50 when she discovered the cancer. She found it herself and her friend encouraged her to have a mammogram from her doctor. She had a mastectomy, but she's great now and she's in her 70s. I am now working with some people in Montgomery, Alabama, and we are trying to form a charity ball to benefit mothers that require breast cancer surgery and are in need of help with their children and have no one else to help. I feel we need to help these women who fall through the cracks of social services. They may have enough income that they don't qualify for help, but who's going to help her child or pay her bills? That's what we are trying to do."

Sister Schubert's breads and cookbook are all products of her dreams.

She reflects on this as she shares, "I've always loved to cook and my dream was to do a cookbook. I've had a very rich background in cooking. I have all these recipes from five generations back. It's not a normal cookbook, because it has stories from my family in it. One of the most special moments I have ever shared with anyone was one afternoon I spent with my grandmother. It's her roll recipe and she taught me how to make these rolls and the trick to making them. It's the way you make the rolls that makes them so good and she taught me the procedure. I give people step by step instructions in the book and walk them through it just like my grandmother walked me through it. She told me how the bread binds your family together. It's true, and when I would make the rolls, my girls would bring all their friends over and they would just sit along the floor with pans of rolls and eat them. Everyone wanted to come to my house! It's a great story about how the bread of our life is so important. When I make bread, I think that I'm passing love to others in the gift of bread."

Sister Schubert is perhaps the "Santa Claus" of the baking industry because of all of the wonderful gifts that she shares. The difference, however, is that she is not simply a spirit of giving, but a real-life example of enthusiasm, compassion, and a heartfelt attitude for life.

finance

Sister Schubert

Attitudes can change your life. That is something that I have noticed by observing the friends in my life. The friends that have maintained good attitudes have been more happy and successful, at anything they have tried to do than the friends that have carried a sour disposition around all of the time. A positive attitude seems to make things easier to deal with by making problems seem smaller than they really are. You can change your attitude by viewing your life in positive tones and destroying your negative outlook. Just look for the good, and watch your songs of anger transform into tunes of happiness and love.
                        —I'm Edie Hand, and that's my attitude for life!

Special Rolls

My favorite food is bread—nice hot bread. Those rolls are a combination of a yeast bread and bread with bakery powder as a leavening agent. Serve with butter or margarine as soon as they come from the oven.

4½	cups flour	2	cups buttermilk
5	teaspoons baking powder	1	cup (2 sticks) butter of margarine
¼	cup sugar	2	packages yeast
1	teaspoon salt		

Blend the first four ingredients together.

Then warm 2 cups buttermilk, and melt 1 cup (2 sticks) butter or margarine. Add margarine and buttermilk to dry mixture. Then add 2 packages yeast—dissolve in ½ cup lukewarm water. Mix well until all dry ingredients are moistened and until dough is blended. Place roll batter on lightly floured surface, kneading several times. Shape into large mounds and let REST for 10 minutes. Roll dough out, and cut with biscuit cutter. Dip each biscuit in very warm melted butter or margarine and place on baking sheet.

Allow to rise and double in size (this can be 30 minutes to 1 hour). Bake at 450° for 20 to 40 minutes (this vary depending on your oven).

Maria Ephraim, Hoover, Alabama

Sister Schubert's Sourdough Rolls

1½ cups warm water (105° to 115°)   6   cups all-purpose flour
1   cup Sourdough Starter (recipe   1   teaspoon salt
    below)   ½   cup butter, melted
½   cup shortening, melted and
    cooled to 105° to 115°

Combine first 3 ingredients in a large bowl. Combine flour and salt in a large bowl. Stir 5 cups of flour mixture into starter mixture. Using your hands, incorporate remaining 1 cup flour mixture. Cover loosely, and let rise in a warm place (85°), free from drafts, for 8 hours.

Grease 4, 8"-round cakepans; set aside.

Punch dough down; turn out onto a well-floured surface, and knead 10 times. Divide dough in half.

Roll 1 portion of dough to ½-inch thickness; cut into 32 rounds using a floured 2 inch biscuit cutter. Pull each round into an oval, approximately 2½ inches long. Dip 1 side of oval into melted butter. Fold oval in half with buttered side facing out.

For each pan, place the folds of 10 rolls against side of prepared pan, pressing center fronts of rolls together gently to seal. Place 5 rolls in inner circle, and 1 roll in center of pan for a total of 16 rolls per pan. Repeat entire procedure with remaining half of dough.

Cover loosely, and let rise in a warm place, free from drafts, 6 hours or until doubled in bulk.

Preheat oven to 375°. Bake rolls, uncovered, for 15 to 18 minutes or until lightly browned.

Yields 64 rolls

Sourdough Starter:

2   packages active dry yeast   ⅔   cup sugar
1½ cups warm water   3   tablespoons instant potato flakes
    (105° to 115°), divided

Combine yeast and ½ cup warm water in a 1 cup liquid measuring cup; let stand 5 minutes.

Combine yeast mixture, remaining 1 cup warm water, sugar, and potato flakes in a large bowl, stirring until well blended. Cover loosely, and let stand in a warm place (85°), free from drafts, for 8 hours. (Starter is ready to use at this point.) Refrigerate starter after 8 hours.

Feed Sourdough Starter every 3 days with: ⅔   cup sugar
1   cup warm water 105° to 115°   3   tablespoons instant potato flakes

After feeding starter, cover loosely, and let stand in a warm place (85°), free from drafts, for 8 hours. Refrigerate starter after 8 hours.

Sister Schubert, Troy, Alabama,
author of Secret Bread Recipes

Leslie Tumlin's Attitude for Life

Making a living is not the same as making a life.

☙

There are times when something comes along in your life that you think you want no part of—and you end up very grateful that there is a bigger, better plan for your life than what you can see. This scenario happened in January 1995—and I was absolutely sure that this "something" had nothing to offer me or my family, until I chose to take a look—at a friend's request. It was one of those "opportunities" that my husband and I usually ran from.

Our neighbors asked us to come over for coffee and just listen—and because we are such good friends, we said "okay." I told her—before listening, of course—that we would not be interested, we just did not have the time for anything else. That was true. We had owned our own pharmacy business for 18 years, and Mickey worked 70 hours a week to provide a wonderful living for our family. Yet . . . we did not have a "life"—we had no time for each other, and Mickey never saw our children. He was working constantly, and something inside of me knew this really was not a life. We had no time to enjoy family, to choose to do things when we wanted—and we already owned our own business—the "American Dream," right? WRONG! The business owned us.

Just 10 minutes into the "presentation," I could see something, a way to bring in other income, (without me going back to work) so that Mickey could spend at least one day a week at home with his family. Little did I know the bigger picture, the greater plan, in store. This unique venture provided so much "other income," we were able to sell our last drugstore just 2 years later! Now, Mickey is home all the time—so much so, that our teenage daughter, in joking exasperation, (from her Dad's teasing) said to us in the kitchen in the middle of the day one summer, "Isn't there something he can go do?!" As we all laughed, I thought, immediately, *I'm living my dream.*

We have our life back now. Mickey is home, we are all home everyday—together. Mickey not only coaches our son's baseball team, he picks our son up from school everyday—and plays the rest of the afternoon. We go on trips—anytime we choose. Every day feels like vacation.

finance

Our new mission in life is to share with others how they can get their life back. Our culture in America is so fast and furious. We wear our "busy-ness" like a badge of honor. We are just "too busy." It's really sad . . . we are "too busy" to make the time to change our lives, and have all the time we could ever dream of, to spend "as we please"—with our loved ones—and to really enjoy "life."

Dad is home; Mom is home; the kids are joyful. Of course, challenges still abound—that is life. But they are not from stress or financial worries. We have the time to embrace the challenges—and to support and encourage others, along their journey.

Our motto regarding this "Pursuit of the American Dream" is "Making a Living is not the same as making a Life."

me with Leslie Tumlin, Mickey Eldridge, and Roxie Kelley

This unique business has made a profound and dramatic change in our family and in the lives of many others we have had the privilege to share it with. We continue to share with thousands how a "non-traditional" business can give you a wonderful "non-traditional" life! THAT is Real Financial Impact.

The opportunity to be involved with and help other people is truly one of the greatest rewards in life. We thank Pam and Steve for asking us to "listen," and we thank the Lord for guiding us to His bigger picture—His greater plan!

—Leslie Tumlin, Birmingham, Alabama,
senior director, Excel

finance

Gourmet

Life is nothing more than a series of routines that we establish for ourselves. Routines can be good or bad—that is up to you. Plan your routine to waste time, or plan to get out and exercise in the sunshine. Make it your routine to ignore your children, or make it your routine to participate and make a difference in their lives. Basically, if you want a different routine, you have the power to change it. So do it now, and make it your routine to improve your life!

—I'm Edie Hand, and that's my attitude for life!

Please Your Appetite with Poppy Seed Bread

3	cups flour	1½	cups cooking oil
2½	cups sugar	1½	tablespoons poppy seeds
1½	teaspoons baking powder	1½	teaspoons vanilla
1½	teaspoons salt	1½	teaspoons almond flavoring
3	eggs	1½	teaspoons butter flavoring
1½	cups milk		

Mix all ingredients together and beat for 2 minutes. Pour into 2 large greased bread pans. Bake at 350° for 1 hour or until toothpick comes out clean. Pour glaze over breads while hot.

Glaze:

¾	cup sugar	½	teaspoon almond flavoring
¼	orange juice	½	teaspoon butter flavoring
½	teaspoon vanilla		

May be frozen.

Edie Hand

Heart Healthy

Whole-Wheat Treat

3	cups warm water	³/₄	cup nonfat dry milk
2	packages compressed or dry yeast	4	teaspoons salt
2	tablespoons honey		Egg substitute equivalent to 2
3	cups whole-wheat flour		eggs
3¹/₂	cups unbleached all-purpose flour	2	tablespoons acceptable vegetable oil
¹/₂	cup soy flour		Vegetable oil spray
1¹/₂	tablespoons wheat germ		

Place warm water in a large bowl. Add yeast and stir to dissolve. Add honey and let sit 5 minutes.

In a bowl, sift together whole-wheat flour, all-purpose flour, soy flour, wheat germ, and nonfat dry milk. Set aside.

Add salt, egg substitute, and three quarters of flour mixture to the yeast mixture. Beat with an electric mixer for 5 minutes. Add oil and remainder of flour mixture. Continue beating until flour is thoroughly mixed and add additional flour if necessary to make dough stiff enough to handle.

Turn dough onto a floured board and knead until it is smooth and elastic. Place dough in an oiled bowl, turning to coat all sides of the dough with oil. Cover with a clean, damp cloth and let rise in a warm place (about 85°) until doubles in bulk. Punch down, fold over the edges and turn upside down in bowl. Cover and allow to rise for another 20 minutes.

Turn dough onto a lightly floured board. Divide into three equal portions. Fold each into the center to make a smooth, tight ball. Cover with cloth and let rest 10 more minutes.

Lightly spray three 8" x 4" loaf pans with vegetable oil.

Shape dough into three loaves and place in prepared loaf pans. Cover and let rise until doubled in bulk.

Preheat oven to 350°. Bake loaves 50 to 60 minutes.

Remove bread from pans and place on wire racks to cool. If a softer crust is desired, brush tops with margarine while hot.

Makes 3 loaves (16 slices per loaf); Serves 48; 1 slice per serving

a favorite of Edie Hand
as found in American Heart Association Cookbook: 5th Edition

American Women in Radio and Television

Susan Cingari, Dr. Ruth, and Edie

Edie with Katie Couric and Lucille Luongo

The mission of AWRT is to advance the impact of women in the electronic media and allied fields by educating, advocating, and acting as a resource to our members and the industry.

Edie and Sally Jesse Raphael at Waldorf Astoria in New York

Jeffy, Edie, Dr. Judy, and Janet in front of the White House during the AWRT National Convention '98

Millet Muffins with Fresh Corn

¾ cup (scant) packed light brown sugar

1 large egg

⅓ cup safflower or corn oil

1 cup buttermilk

7 tablespoons millet (available in natural food stores)

1⅓ cups unbleached all-purpose flour

1 teaspoon baking powder

1 teaspoon baking soda

¼ teaspoon salt

1 cup plus 1 tablespoon fresh corn kernels

Preheat the oven to 375°. Lightly oil or spray a 12-cup muffin tin with nonstick vegetable oil spray. Beat the sugar and egg together until smooth. Add the oil and ½ cup of the buttermilk and stir until well blended. Using a food processor, blender, or mortar and pestle, grind the millet until it is the coarseness of kosher salt. Whisk the flour with the baking powder, baking soda, and salt. Add the millet and whisk several times to blend. Add the dry ingredients and combine with a few swift strokes. Add the remaining ½ cup of buttermilk and the corn kernels and mix well with a rubber spatula. Spoon the batter into the muffin cups, filling each one about two-thirds full. Bake for about 22 minutes, until lightly browned and risen. The tops may crack, which is acceptable, and a toothpick inserted in the center of a muffin should come out clean. Cool slightly and then turn out of the muffin tin onto wire racks to cool completely. Serve at room temperature.

Serves 4

a favorite of Edie Hand
as found in Heart Healthy Cooking for All Seasons

Jane Pauley and Edie at AWRT luncheon at the Waldorf in New York in the 80s

Edie with Barbara Walters at an American Women in Radio and Television event

I Miss Elvis Presley

One step begins a journey,
One note begins a song,
Once in every life time,
A legend comes along.
A star from Memphis, shone
so bright.
Like a diamond in the sky.
The king was called, before
his time,
But his song will never die.
I miss Elvis Presley,
But there's one thing we can
do,
We can love him tender,
We can love him true.
He can't be here with us,
But deep within my soul,

I believe that he would want
For us to know,
That he should be remem-
bered,
For the gift he gave—the
song.
And his music lives forever,
Even though the king is
gone.
Now he's come and gone.
Didn't stay that long.
The man from Mississippi,
Sure could sing a song.

—by David Austin and
Jon Park Wheeler,
performed by The Jordanaires

The Jordanaires with Edie in Collingwood,
Canada, at an Elvis tribute event

family

parenting

*N*o one is more important in your child's life than you. And, no one knows more about parenting than John Croyle, founder of the Big Oak Boys and Girls Ranches, a safe haven for battered and neglected children. John shares these tips for successful parenting: "As parents, our job is to prepare our children for the journey called life. To really put it into perspective, we have 18 years to pack our children's bags. When they turn 18 and graduate from high school, we are practically through at that point. When that child goes out into the world, reality is waiting to take a chunk out of their young backside. If we don't prepare our children, they probably won't make it.

"Your child's future hinges on the experiences they have with you. You can give them the finest of everything from a home, to clothes and a car, and all the money they need, *but,* if you haven't invested in their heart to have a real commitment to God, you have left out the most essential characteristic. In addition to that understanding, there are only two things your child has to have from you to make it in this world: Number one, they've got to know you love them. And number two, they've got to know you believe in them."

Thanks to John Croyle for sharing that insight into parenting.

Linc's first tv commercial, 1986. Sharing in mom's work life—Fun Quality Time!

Main Dishes

Winter Carnival Casserole

2	tablespoons corn oil	1/2	teaspoon chili powder
1/4	cup onion, finely chopped	1/4	teaspoon pepper
1/4	cup green pepper, finely chopped	1	bay leaf
1	pound ground beef	2	tablespoons corn starch
1	12-ounce can tomatoes and juice	3	cups cooked macaroni or rice
1/2	cup of karo all-purpose syrup	1	cup shredded sharp cheddar cheese
1/2	teaspoon salt		

Heat corn oil in skillet. Add chopped onion and green pepper and cook until tender. Add ground beef; brown, stirring often. Pour out and save 1/4 cup liquid from the tomatoes. Add all of the tomatoes, karo syrup, salt, chili powder, pepper, and bay leaf to meat mixture. Bring to boil, cover and simmer for 15 minutes. Blend corn starch with the tomato liquid; stir into the meat mixture. Bring to boil, stirring. Add macaroni or rice; pour into a 2-quart casserole. Sprinkle with shredded cheese. Bake in a 350° oven about 30 minutes.

Makes 6 delicious servings

Jean B. Williams, Jasper, Alabama

Eye Opening Breakfast Pizza

1	pound pork sausage
1	8-count package crescent rolls
1	cup frozen hash browns
1	cup shredded sharp cheddar cheese
2	tablespoons Parmesan cheese, grated
3	eggs
1/4	cup milk
1/2	teaspoon salt
1/8	teaspoon pepper

Cook sausage until brown and crumbly; drain. Separate dough into 8 triangles. Place on ungreased 12"-pizza pan with points to center. Press over bottom, sealing edge, and pressing up sides. Spoon sausage on dough. Sprinkle on thawed potatoes. Top with cheddar cheese. Beat eggs with milk, salt, and pepper. Pour evenly over pizza. Sprinkle Parmesan cheese on top. Bake at 375° for 25 to 30 minutes.

Michele Smith, Blountsville, Alabama

Melba Wolverton's Attitude for Life

There's no miracle for losing weight. My overall attitude is persistence. You have to do whatever it takes to get the job done.

Ꭶ

Some people may never guess that a chief nursing officer and operations coordinator, as well as a registered nurse and the owner of a wellness center, would ever have a problem controlling her own health issues. For Melba Wolverton, however, this was not the case. This bubbly, energetic owner of the Jasper Wellness Image Center was not always in control of the health in her life. In fact, she almost took her own life as a result of her unhappiness.

She remembers this time in her life because it was a major turning point in her self-esteem, her attitude, and her career: "I now diet and exercise and that has changed my whole attitude. I began doing it for emotional reasons, but, of course, the weight was a secondary cause. I was at a point in my life where everything was going to start going downhill because of my weight. I didn't feel good about myself because it was the whole image thing. I felt that people couldn't get past the weight. How does somebody think you're together if you weigh 255 pounds? It's like going to a hairdresser to get your hair done and her hair is burned or frizzed. I was to the point where I could have committed suicide, because I decided that my life was not going to go on like this. Everything was changing. My marriage was ending and I wouldn't want to call attention to myself at work because I didn't feel good about myself."

It was at this point that Melba decided that she had to make some changes.

"I had gone to my doctor and told him I wanted to lose this weight. They gave me a 1,000- to 1,200-calorie a day diet, and that was a major change, but I went on it. In 6 months I had lost 65 pounds. It took 9 months to a year to lose the 100 pounds. I felt skinny then, so I would take breaks, but you have to in order to not burn out. Treat yourself periodically. You cannot take off that much weight without exercising. Plus, you don't want wrinkles with all of the loose skin. Regardless of me losing all that weight, I still had cellulite and big hips and legs. I tried everything, and then I decided on liposuction. This did nothing for the cellulite, though, and it

fitness

Melba, before, and after her weight loss with her fiancé

left the skin wrinkled. It really did not shape my legs like I wanted, so I began cellulite therapy treatments on the machines at the wellness center in Florence, Alabama. I started seeing phenomenal results. In nine treatments, I lost 5¼ inches and in eighteen, 10¼. These are non-invasive treatments on the subdermal layer of tissue. I did it two to three times a week and it's the first thing that has ever reduced my thighs."

Not only does Melba continue the treatments now, but she has now opened her own wellness center in her hometown of Jasper, Alabama.

She said, "It's a maintenance thing. I do it at least once a month and it's wonderful. I've lost 10¼ inches since I started at the wellness center. In order to be successful at losing weight, you've got to make a commitment and know it's not easy. There's no miracle for losing, but there's products that can help you. Then find a diet that works for you. Drink 6 to 8 glasses of water a day and do at least 3 days of aerobic exercise and a little bit of weight lifting because muscle burns calories.

When you get tired, it's a habit to eat for energy, so try to avoid this and get plenty of rest. Candy doesn't do it, and neither does caffeine and sugar, because you crash when your blood sugar drops. Don't leave out any of the food groups. I feel great when I take care of myself. I have the center because I want to take this to other people."

Melba continues to share that dream by not only helping others, but serving as an inspirational example to those that are also struggling with their weight. Melba not only found a new self-esteem and an addition to her career, but she found a new attitude. And that has made all the difference.

Melba Wolverton's Guide for a Healthier, Thinner You

It is important to:
- Reach and stay at a reasonable weight.
- Be careful of serving sizes.
- Avoid skipping meals.
- Increase your daily activity.
- Eat less fat.
- Eat smaller servings of meat. Eat fish and poultry more often. Choose lean cuts of red meat.
- Prepare all meats by roasting, baking, or broiling. Trim off all fat. Be careful of added sauces or gravy. Remove skin from poultry.
- Avoid fried foods. Avoid adding fat in cooking.
- Eat fewer high-fat foods such as cold cuts, bacon, sausage, hot dogs, butter, margarine, nuts, salad dressing, lard, and solid shortening.
- Drink skim or low-fat milk.
- Eat less ice cream, cheese, sour cream, cream, whole milk, and other high-fat dairy products.
- Eat more high fiber foods.
- Choose dried beans, peas and lentils more often.
- Eat whole grain breads, cereals, and crackers.
- Eat more vegetables, both raw and cooked.
- Eat whole fruit in place of fruit juice.
- Try other high fiber foods, such as oat bran, barley, bulgur, brown rice, or wild rice.
- Reduce the amount of salt you use in cooking.

fitness

- Try not to put salt on food at the table.
- Eat fewer high-salt foods, such as canned soups, ham, sauerkraut, hot dogs, pickles, and foods that taste salty.
- Eat fewer convenience and fast foods.
- Eat less sugar.
- Avoid regular soft drinks. One 12-ounce can has nine teaspoons of sugar.
- Avoid eating table sugar, honey, syrup, jam, jelly, candy, sweet rolls, fruit canned in syrup, regular gelatin desserts, cake with icing, pie or other sweets.
- Choose fresh fruit or fruit canned in natural juice or water.
- If desired, use sweeteners that don't have any calories, such as saccharin or aspartame, instead of sugar.

Example Daily Diet

Breakfast:	2 breads	*Supper:*	2 oz. meat
	1 meat		1 bread
	1 fruit		1 vegetable
	1 milk		1 fruit
	1 fat		1 fat
Lunch:	2 oz. meat	*Snack Time:*	1 milk
	2 breads	*(Bedtime)*	1 fruit
	1 vegetable		
	1 fat		

Each day you need to eat a variety of foods. Each person's daily calorie and nutritional needs are different. A nutrition counselor can help you work out how many choices from each food group are just right for you. For a healthy diet, each day you have at least 4 choices from the starch/bread group, 5 meat or meat substitute choices, 2 vegetable choices, 2 fruit choices, 2 skim milk choices, and not more than 3 fat choices. These choices add up to about 1,200 calories per day.

Examples:
- starch/bread   ½ cup pasta or barley
⅓ cup rice or cooked dried beans and peas
1 small potato (½ cup mashed)
½ cup starchy vegetables
1 slice bread or 1 roll
½ English muffin, bagel, or bun

fitness

½ cup cooked cereal
¾ cup dry cereal
3 cups popcorn, unbuttered and not cooked in oil
- vegetables
½ cup cooked vegetables
1 cup raw veggies
½ cup tomato/vegetable juice
- milk
1 cup skim milk
6-8 oz. carton plain lowfat yogurt
- meat and substitutes
1 oz. cooked poultry, fish or meat
¼ cup cottage cheese
¼ cup salmon or tuna, water packed
1 tablespoon peanut butter
1 egg
1 oz. low-fat cheese, such as Mozzarella
- 2 meats/substitutes
1 small chicken leg or thigh
½ cup cottage cheese or tuna
- 3 meats/substitutes
1 small pork chop
1 small hamburger
½ of a whole chicken breast
1 medium fish fillet
- fruit
1 fresh medium fruit
1 cup berries or melon
½ cup canned in juice or w/out sugar
½ cup fruit juice
¼ cup dried fruit
- fat
1 teaspoon margarine, oil, mayonnaise
2 teaspoons diet margarine or diet mayonnaise
1 tablespoon salad dressing
2 tablespoons reduced-calorie salad dressing

fitness

Happy Hash Brown Quiche

1   24-ounce package
    frozen hash brown
    potatoes, thawed
1/3 cup melted butter or
    margarin e
1   cup shredded hot
    pepper cheese
1/2 cup shredded Swiss
    cheese
1/2 cup shredded Cheddar
    cheese
1   cup diced cooked ham
1/2 cup cream or milk
2   eggs
1/4 teaspoon seasoned salt

Press thawed potatoes between paper towels and fit into greased 9" or 10" quiche pan. Brush with melted butter and bake at 425° for 30 minutes. Remove from oven and fill with cheeses and ham. Beat cream, eggs, and salt together and pour over all. Bake at 350° for 30 minutes.

Melba Wolverton, Jasper, Alabama

Tongue!

1   3-pound beef tongue
2   teaspoons salt
3   bay leaves
6   whole allspice
3   whole black peppers
3   onions, sliced
1   stalk celery
1   cup cider vinegar
2   tablespoons garlic,
    minced

Wash tongue; cover with hot water; add seasonings and vegetables; cook slowly, about 3 hours. Cool in liquid. Trim excess tissue from root end and remove skin.

Slice and serve with horseradish sauce or chutney.

Makes 8 servings

This recipe was my mom's favorite. We took tongue sandwiches to school and frightened our friends!
Glenna Salsbury, CSP, CPAE, Paradise Valley, Arizona, past national president, National Speakers Association

Until further notice, celebrate everything.
—Tim Hansel

Baked Chicken

You'll need 8 chicken breasts—take a Corningware pan and line it with tin foil and sprinkle with salt and pepper then place the chicken breasts in the pan and sprinkle flour over the chicken. Put a small slice of butter or margarine on each piece. Pour a little water in the pan. Cook at 300° for 20, minutes then bake at 250° for about 2 hours or until done so as not to get dry. Check every 30 minutes and open the foil when needed to brown the top of the chicken breast.

Connie Hopper,
Southern gospel singer

Connie Hopper and her singing gospel family

Seize every moment you have in life with your family and serve the Lord with the talents he has given you.

—*Connie Hopper*

Mary Tom's Mexican Chicken

½   pound bag Doritos, crushed

3   cans Swanson Chicken

2   cans Cream of Chicken soup

1   cup sour cream

1   can chopped green chilies

1   tablespoon onion, chopped

Place crushed Doritos in casserole dish. Place chicken on top of crushed doritos. Mix all ingredients together and pour over Doritos. Sprinkle cheese on top and bake at 425° for 20 minutes or until cheese melts.

Mary Tom Speer Reid, Nashville, Tennessee,
of the legendary Speer Family of gospel music

Dolly's Meatloaf

1½ pounds ground sirloin
    (or other lean meat)
½   cup ketchup
½   cup tomato juice
2   eggs, beaten
¾   cup fresh bread crumbs
½   cup onions, finely
    chopped
2   teaspoons prepared
    mustard
½   teaspoon salt
½   teaspoon pepper
    Green pepper and/or
    celery (optional)

Mix all ingredients together with hands and put in baking dish. Bake at 400° about 1 hour (or until desired done-ness). After baking for 45 minutes, pour extra ketchup on top and continue to bake.

NOTE: Best served with mashed potatoes, creamed corn, and apple pie.

Dolly Parton,
Country music legend

Dolly Parton—"workin' 9 to 5" and still has time to fix her famous meatloaf

People are just about as happy as they make up their minds to be.
—Abraham Lincoln

Tasty Taco Pie

2	pounds ground beef
1	can refried beans
1	package taco seasoning
1	package flour tortillas
8	ounces Mozzarella cheese

Brown hamburger meat and drain fat. Add taco seasoning and water according to package directions. Add refried beans and simmer for 10 minutes. In a 9" x 13" pan, layer soft shells and mixture two times. Top with cheese. Bake 10 to 15 minutes in a 250° oven. Top with lettuce, tomato, taco sauce, and sour cream if desired.

Betty Odom, Curry, Alabama

Mexican Treasure Casserole

1	pound ground beef
1	package dry chili mix
1	can tomatoes
1-2	packages yellow rice
1	can cheddar cheese soup
1/2	cup milk

Brown and drain ground beef, add chili mix and tomatoes, and simmer for 30 minutes, stirring occasionally. Prepare rice according to package directions. In large casserole dish, layer rice and beef mixture. Combine cheese soup with milk and heat. Pour over meat and rice. Bake at 350° for 30 minutes. Garnish with chopped onion, tomatoes, shredded cheese, shredded lettuce, and taco chips. Use taco sauce is desired. Delicious!!!

Angela Lockhart, Jasper, Alabama

Cheesy Grits Casserole

1	cup grits (quick or regular)
1/2	cup margarine
3	eggs, beaten
2/3	cup sweet milk
1/2	pound Cheddar cheese
1/2	pound fried bacon, crumbled (optional)

Cook grits according to package instructions. Add margarine to hot grits and stir until margarine is melted. Add cheese and stir. Combine eggs with milk and stir into grits. Add crumbled bacon. Pour into greased 2-quart casserole dish. Sprinkle extra cheese on top if you desire. Bake 30 to 40 minutes at 325° until mixture is set and lightly browned. (The center is the last to cook.)

Jackie Parker, Dora, Alabama

Luscious Lemon Pepper Chicken

1   bag frozen broccoli
1   bag frozen stir fry
    vegetables (any mix
    will do that has a bit of
    onion, diced carrots,
    snap peas, etc.)
1-2 pounds skinless chicken
    breasts
    Mustard
    Lemon pepper

Mix the vegetables together and place in a large baking pan. Put chicken breasts on top of this and coat with mustard and then sprinkle with lemon pepper. Bake at 350° until chicken is done. Serve with rice.

Janet Noll, Raleigh, North Carolina,
national board member,
American Women in Radio and Television

The Easiest Crock Pot Roast in the World

3   pound roast
1   envelope onion soup
    mix
4-5 potatoes, chopped
5-6 carrots, chopped

Put roast in crock pot. Top with onion soup mix and cover with potatoes and carrots. Set crock pot on low and let cook 8 or more hours.

Natalie Farr, Honey Grove, Texas

Southern Fried Salmon Patties

1   can pink salmon
    Salt
    Pepper
¼   cup white onion, diced
2   eggs
    Milk
2   tablespoons of flour
    Oil

Drain can of salmon, then remove all skin and as many bones as possible. Mash salmon up really good and add lots of pepper and some salt. Add ¼ cup of diced onion, 2 eggs, and 2 tablespoons of flour, and mix well with the salmon. Add just enough milk to the mixture for the patties to hold together when frying. Have your skillet almost ½ full with oil and on medium-high heat. Spoon patties into hot pan and flip when brown on one side. Taste light and everyone will love them.

Pam Lindley Jarrett, Addison, Alabama

Rise 'n Shine Orange Ring

1   cup sugar
3   tablespoons orange
    rind, grated
2   12-ounce cans
    refrigerator buttermilk
    biscuits
1/3 cup butter or
    margarine, melted
1   3-ounce package cream
    cheese, softened
1/2 cup sifted, powdered
    sugar
2   tablespoons orange
    juice

Combine sugar and orange rind. Separate biscuits; dip each in butter and coat with sugar mixture. Stand biscuits on sides, overlapping edges, in a 9" tube pan. Bake at 350° for 30 minutes or until golden brown. Remove ring from pan and invert on a serving platter. Combine cream cheese and powdered sugar, mixing until smooth. Add orange juice, stirring well; spoon over top of ring while ring is hot. Serve bread warm.

Toni Drummond, Jasper, Alabama

*Having fun cruising New York
with Toni and Carolyn Drummond*

Golden Olympic Reuben Sandwiches

Tailgating is a big thing at the Smith household. Packing up the truck with our favorite goodies and heading down on the plains to watch Auburn football is our favorite pastime. Here's what I like to see in our picnic basket on football weekends in the loveliest village on the plains.

1   cup Thousand Island
    dressing
12 slices bread (your
    choice)
12 slices Swiss cheese
1/2 cup sauerkraut, drained
24 slices of corned beef,
    thinly sliced
    Margarine

Spread 1/2 cup of dressing on one side of 6 slices of bread. Arrange 1 slice cheese, 2 teaspoons sauerkraut, and 2 slices of the corned beef evenly on each slice. Spread remaining 1/2 cup of dressing on remaining 6 slices of bread. Wrap in aluminum foil and bake for 20 minutes at 325° or place on a grill until hot.

*Willie Smith, Birmingham, Alabama,
3-time Olympic Gold Medal winner*

Willie Smith's Attitude for Life

After interviewing Willie Smith for only a few minutes, I found him to be an admirable man. As an Olympic gold medalist, loving father, and husband, Willie Smith has shown the world how hard work and perseverance will triumph in the end.

Willie remembers his beginnings, "In 1968, on California Avenue at my elementary school during a field day, I began running. It was also the first time I fell down during a relay race. The second time in 1976, it cost the United States a gold medal."

This would not be the only time in Willie's life that he would pick himself up and move on. Willie recounts his feeling of disappointment when, after years of training, he was unable to go to the Olympics because of the U.S. boycott in 1980. Willie said, "I had such a disappointment in the 1976 Olympics. I had trained for four years after that, so I knew I was ready for the '80 Olympics and fully prepared for the start-up.

"I had done all the right things. I had graduated from Auburn and dreamed of being an American Olympic hero in 1980. It was in August or September that we began hearing rumors that then President Jimmy Carter was considering a U.S. boycott of the 1980 Summer Olympics in Moscow because of the U.S.S.R.'s invasion of Afghanistan. Nobody believed it or wanted to believe it, but by early winter it was official. Nevertheless, I kept training. I thought something was going to change before the spring. I got second in the Olympic trials, but the officials said that I was not going. Nobody was going.

"That put everything on hold for us. I went back to Auburn after the boycott.

"For a long time, I couldn't find the strength to continue training. It was like something had been placed in my path. I thought that maybe I should go back for the 1984 Olympics, but I couldn't find any direction. I sat around watching soap operas. Then reality hit. I was not getting any younger. The 1984 Olympics would be my last chance. I married in 1982 and took a position in sports medicine at Samford University in Birmingham. They also promised to help me get back to the '84 Olympics. With a renewed spirit and encouragement from my wife, my quest for the '84 Olympics began. At age 28, 6 years

fitness

(left to right): Harvey Glama, head track coach, University of Alabama, Edie, and Willie Smith

older than any other competitor, I made the Olympic
team, finishing fifth in the trials. Although I was an alternate, I
ran in the first two rounds of the preliminaries and in the semi-
finals. It was my job to help the 400 meter relay team to get to
the finals. It was very exciting for me to compete in those races,
but I had to sit and watch the team compete and win in the
finals. I had done my part and I also received my Olympic gold
medal.

   "I might not have been part of the '84 Olympic team had it
not been for John Woods of AmSouth Bank. I sent him a letter
stating that I needed further sponsorship in order to compete. I
soon received a check for $3,000.00 in the mail. Not only that,
but they set me up on a circuit, speaking to schools about my
experiences and about the Olympics and training. I talked also
about the longevity of the sport; how people can stay fit
throughout their life and feel great. I have been involved in staying fit all of my life. I competed as a sprinter in the '84 Olympics
when many people considered me "too old." Even 4 years after
the Olympics, I could run faster than I did when I won the gold
medal. Fitness has always been, and will be, a major part of my
life. I continue to work with young people to improve not only
their physical fitness, but their mental fitness as well. You can't

fitness

have success in one without the other. The ancient Greeks believed in a sound body and a sound mind. I do, too.

"I have been my own worst enemy. Fear of success brought me down because success brought with it responsibility. I didn't know what to do with all the things that came with being a star."

Willie Smith has overcome many obstacles in his life and has conquered them by holding onto his dreams, even when they seemed out of reach. Not only has he held onto those dreams, but he shares them with his family. According to Willie, there is no greater supporter of his dreams than his wife, Donna. Together, Willie and Donna are passing on the dreams and lessons to their daughter, Kendal. Kendal's goal is to one day earn a college track scholarship and hopefully run in the Olympics. Kendal says that true dedication to a sport can be tough and it takes a special type of person. Luckily for her, she has a mentor in her father. Willie Smith has come a long way from that little boy who fell down in elementary school. He is now an example to the world of how perseverance makes you a winner.

Willie Smith dining with his family— wife, Donna, and daughter, Kendal

fitness

Ben's Spaghetti and Meat Sauce

2   tablespoons butter
½   medium onion,
     chopped
1½   pounds ground round
     Italian seasoning taste
     Salt and pepper to taste
     Garlic salt to taste
1-2 16-ounce cans tomato
     sauce
1   16-ounce can tomato
     juice

In a skillet, melt the butter and sauté the onion. Add the ground round and cook until the meat is well done. Drain the fat off the meat and add the Italian seasoning, salt, pepper, and garlic salt to taste. Add the tomato sauce and can of tomato juice (you can throw in another can of tomato juice, depending on how thick you like your sauce). Cover and simmer for 15 to 30 minutes. Serve over spaghetti, angel hair, or your choice of pasta. Serves 4 to 6

Ben Speer
of the legendary gospel group,
The Speer Family, and
director, Ben Speer's Stamps-
Baxter School of Music,
as found in
The Presley Family
and Friends Cookbook

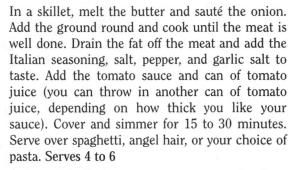

Ben Speer, Mr. and Mrs. James Blackwood, and Edie at Brock and Faye Speers 50th Anniversary Party in Nashville

Road Kill Omelet for Four

12   large eggs
½   cup of milk
1   medium size tomato
½   bell pepper
½   medium size onion
½   pound of fresh road kill
     (deer, opossum, or
     squirrel) or, if that is
     not available, ham will
     suffice

Prepare all ingredients before heating large skillet. Beat eggs thoroughly and add ½ cup of milk to eggs. Chop all other ingredients to about the size of a double-ought buckshot. Heat skillet to medium and pour in eggs. After eggs have cooked for about 1 minute, add all other ingredients. After adding the above, let cook on low heat for 1 minute. Then fold omelet and turn off heat. Serve omelet directly from skillet.

Note: When preparing this recipe at a condominium on beach location, you might want to combine all ingredients at once and stir while cooking until ready to serve.

Jerry Sowards, Germantown, Tennessee,
bass singer, Homeland Quartet

Neici's Chicken n' Dumplins

This recipe will cure anything from a bad day to a bad cold!

1   chicken
1½ cups water
2   cups all-purpose flour
1   egg
½ teaspoon baking powder
1   teaspoon margarine
    Salt to taste
½ teaspoon pepper

Pressure cook 1 chicken and debone. Save the chicken broth and put aside. Mix together all other ingredients. Roll flat and cut into long pieces. Let set no longer then 1 hour. Bring left over chicken broth to a boil. Drop all pieces into chicken broth, add deboned chicken, and let simmer for 15 minutes.

Cherina Rice, Germantown, Tennessee

Country Captain Chicken

1   3-pound chicken, skin removed
½ cup flour
1   tablespoon salt
¼ teaspoon pepper
¼ cup shortening
1   cup onions, chopped
1   cup green pepper, chopped
1   garlic clove, minced
1½ cups water
1   14-ounce bottle ketchup
½ teaspoon curry powder
½ teaspoon ground thyme
    Several cups hot, cooked rice
⅓ dried currants
½ cup toasted, blanched almonds, chopped

Heat oven to 350°. Cut up chicken and coat with mixture of flour, salt, and pepper. In Dutch oven or roaster, brown chicken in shortening. Remove from pan. Sauté onion, pepper, and garlic until lightly browned. Add water, ketchup, curry, and thyme, and mix well. Add chicken, coating each piece with sauce and cover. Bake 1 hour, stirring occasionally. Serve chicken surrounded by rice. Add currants to sauce and pour over chicken. Sprinkle with almonds.

Serves 6

Jean B. Williams, Jasper, Alabama

Louisiana Corn Creole

1   pound lean hamburger
    meat
1   medium onion
1   medium bell pepper
1   can cream style corn
½   cup milk
1   egg, beaten
½   cup corn meal
1   can Cream of Chicken
    soup
1   cup grated cheese
    (or ½ pound)

Brown hamburger meat, onion, and bell pepper all together. Add cream style corn; cook for 1 minute. Add milk and egg beaten together; cook for another minute. Then add corn meal and cook for 1 minute. Pour into a large casserole dish. Spread Cream of Chicken over top (add a little water if necessary) and then sprinkle grated cheese over top). Bake at 350° for 30 minutes.

Patty Barrett, Gadsden, Alabama

Chicken Casserole

    Ritz or Escort crackers
1   stick butter or
    margarine, melted
6   chicken breasts, boiled
    and chopped
1   can Cream of Chicken
    soup
1   can Cream of
    Mushroom soup
1   carton sour cream
    poppy seeds

Layer cracker crumbs in bottom of casserole. Pour part of butter over them. Mix cooked, boned chicken, soups, and sour cream; pour over crumbs. Top with cracker crumbs and pour remaining butter over crumbs. Sprinkle poppy seeds on top. Bake for 30 minutes at 350°.

Serves 6

Barbara W. Cashion, Red Bay, Alabama,
Edie's special high school teacher

my favorite teacher from high school, Barbara W. Cashion

Crock Pot Brunswick Stew

1   whole chicken, cooked
    and boned
2   cans Castleberry
    barbecue pork (3-
    sandwich size)
1   small onion, chopped
1   small can cream style
    corn
1   can shoe peg corn
1   small can green lima
    beans
2   cans crushed tomatoes
1   large potato, boiled and
    mashed
3-4 tablespoons ketchup
3-4 tablespoons
    Worcestershire sauce

Combine all ingredients in a crock pot. Cook on low about 12 to 24 hours. The longer it cooks, the better.

Linda Lewis, Jasper, Alabama,
Chamber of Commerce of Walker County

with radio- and TV-legend Ralph Emery

Loving Life Lasagna

1   pound Jimmy Dean
     Sage sausage
1/4 teaspoon garlic powder
1   tablespoon basil
1   teaspoon salt
1   1-pound can crushed
     tomatoes
2   6-ounce cans tomato
     paste
8   lasagna noodles
2   cups low fat cottage
     cheese
1/2 cup shredded Parmesan
     cheese
2   tablespoons parsley
     flakes
2   eggs, beaten
1   teaspoon salt
1/2 teaspoon pepper
1   pound Mozzarella
     cheese, sliced thinly

Brown sausage slowly, spooning off excess fat. Add next five ingredients. Simmer, uncovered, 30 minutes, stirring occasionally. Cook noodles in a large amount of boiling, salted water until tender. Drain and rinse noodles. Combine remaining ingredients, except Mozzarella cheese. Place half the noodles in 13" x 9" x 2" baking dish; spread with half the cottage cheese filling; add half the Mozzarella cheese as a layer; spread half the meat sauce over the cheese layer. Repeat layers. Bake in a preheated 350° oven 30 minutes. Let stand 10 minutes before cutting.

Makes 12 servings

Ralph Emery, Nashville, Tennessee,
talk show host and producer of The Ralph Emery Show
and author of The View from Nashville

Ralph Emery's Attitude for Life

The word "no" in most cases is not an option.
"No" just gets in the way of progress.

∽

A person can't earn the title of "the Dick Clark of country music" or "the Johnny Carson of cable TV" without being very talented and very persistent. In fact, Ralph Emery credits the strength behind his success as his strong will to survive and his unwillingness to accept the word "no." It's this strong will and ambition that has exemplified Ralph Emery's attitude for life.

He says, "It may be true that sometimes some things may not work, but I guess I like to find that out the hard way. I have done that in many cases. Perseverance, I guess, is worth more than anything else to any individual in any field if he or she is willing to hang tough. You get your feelings hurt a lot and just roll with the punches. I watched Bruce Jenner do a piece a while back and he was talking about the fact that success is not a straight line because it has so many ups and downs. So, your line may go up and down, and down and up. No matter what you achieve in life, there will be peaks and valleys along the way."

Anyone who has been around Ralph long enough can easily tell that there is an abundance of fun just waiting to leap from his soul. It may be that he is just telling a story or wearing "billy bob" teeth with Ray Stevens, but it is obvious that this man knows how to have a good time.

"I do anything to get attention. I was an overnight DJ for years on WSM radio. Ten o'clock at night to 5:00 in the morning was my shift, and I used to worry that I would put people to sleep or I would bore them to death. I used to think to myself that it would be awful to be there at 2:00 A.M. and have nobody listen. So, I came up with a lot of off-the-wall things to keep listeners interested. I think in that case, it worked. Yeah, I think I'm a fun-loving person."

fun

When Ralph and his wife want to kick back and have fun, they try their hands at golf. "I tried to get my wife interested in golf, which is a passion for me. You talk about not wanting to take no for an answer. Well, golf is probably the most humiliating game that man has ever devised! You can look at a paper and find that the same championship golfers do not win every weekend. It is because it's a game that you cannot blame anyone else for the way you hit the ball. It's a mind game. Someone said that golf is played between the ears, and he is right. And, because there are so many variations in the game, you can play this golf course out here and the ball will never land in the same place as it landed the last time you played. So, you calculate differently as to how you're going to reach the green and which golf club you will use. But I love the game, and after all these years of being humiliated, I can tell you to pursue it. I tried to interest my wife, Joy, this past summer and did for a short while. I think that she found she doesn't like it that well. Joy loves dancing and I have two left feet, so I don't accommodate her very well. But we love traveling together and we have done extensive traveling."

Ralph is not only the proud owner of golf clubs, but the proud father of 3 sons, the grandfather of several grandchildren, and the great-grandfather of 1.

"My oldest granddaughter is a nurse practitioner and I have recently become a great grandfather. The baby's name is Emma Clair and we try to avoid calling her Eclair. My youngest son is married to a special education teacher, who's getting her Master's degree. He just graduated from college. My middle son is a chemist and is getting married in May. We recently started a family tradition in the last 2 or 3 years. On Thanksgiving morning we go to the Springhouse and I play golf with my three boys and then we have lunch at the Springhouse's Thanksgiving buffet. You can have anything you want!"

fun

Ralph sums up his recipe for life by saying that he tries not to get upset about very much.

"Roll with the punches! Most of the things that you worry about never happen. I think I developed my attitude when I was doing live television way back. No matter what happened on the set, I would not lose control. What makes me tick is that I am one of those people who get out and ring the bell and shout for country music. Mike Reed, an all-American at Penn State and a player for the Bengals, came to Nashville and had the best answer I ever heard to the question of why country music is so popular. He said, 'I think country music is popular because it has the faith to tell everyone that their problems are important, and that flows into everything else you do.' What they do and think may not seem important to us, but it's important to them. My attitude is influenced by my wife and sometimes it changes. I don't like to be around negative people. Bad vibes bring me down, and I don't want to be brought down. Johnny Carson always said, 'Don't tell people your problems. Ninety percent will be glad you have them and the other 10 percent won't care.' I keep doing what I'm doing because I like it and I don't know how to do anything else. I enjoy all of the people that I work with and I have a great curiosity in finding out how others find the strength to achieve their goals. I have always enjoyed my work. One day I was driving down West End Avenue and I thought, *I am tired of doing this.* Then I kept driving and thinking, then realized, *I don't know how to do anything else.*"

Ralph Emery may say that he knows how to do nothing else, but he definitely knows how to make whatever he does a complete success. The word "no" doesn't hinder Ralph Emery. It's just a little tidbit on the golfing green of life.

fun

Chicken with a Ring!

4	chicken breasts without skin
1	tablespoon butter
1½	cups shredded Monterey Jack cheese
1	can onion rings
½	cup mushrooms (optional)

Cook chicken breasts in oven at 350° for 30 minutes. In a casserole dish, place chicken, butter, cheese, and onion rings. Bake for 8 to 10 minutes more until cheese melts.
   Delicious!

Brenda Lawson, Birmingham, Alabama

Down Home Chuck Roast

3	pounds chuck roast
1	cup all purpose flour
1	10¾-once can Golden Mushroom soup
1	6-ounce package dry onion soup mix
2	soup cans water
	Sliced potatoes, optional
	Sliced onions, optional
	Sliced carrots, optional

Preheat the oven to 350°. Rub the flour over the chuck roast. In a cast iron skillet, brown the meat over medium heat. Add the remaining ingredients, and then bake for 1 hour and 30 minutes to 2 hours. You may add potatoes, onion, and carrots during the last 30 minutes of cooking.

Serves 6

Kim Blackburn Poss, Tuscumbia, Alabama, sister of Edie Hand

Beefy Barbecue Hamburgers

1½	to 2 pounds lean ground chuck
1	cup quick oats
1	small onion, chopped
	Pinch salt
	Pinch pepper
	Pinch garlic powder
1	12-ounce can evaporated milk
1	15-ounce bottle barbecue sauce

In a large bowl, mix the meat, oats, onion, salt, pepper, and garlic powder. Add the milk and stir well. Shape the meat into patties. In a skillet, brown the patties on both sides. Cover with your favorite barbecue sauce and let simmer for 45 minutes. You may have to add a little water while it cooks. This can be made in advance, left in the sauce, and reheated later.

Serves 6

Linc Hand, Dora, Alabama, Edie Hand's son

Vegetarian Lasagna

1	16-ounce carton light ricotta cheese
1	egg
1	cup medium onions, chopped
2	cloves garlic
2	tablespoons olive oil
1/2	cup celery, chopped
1/2	cup green pepper, chopped
1	tablespoon sugar
1	15-ounce can tomatoes
1	8-ounce can tomato paste
	Oregano
1	bunch parsley, chopped
	Precooked lasagna noodles
4	cups (1 pound) grated or sliced Mozzarella cheese
1/2	cup Parmesan cheese, grated
1	pound fresh spinach, cleaned and chopped
1	cup fresh tomatoes, chopped
	Basil
	Thyme

In a medium bowl, mix the ricotta and egg together for easier spreading. Make the tomato mixture by sautéing the onions and garlic in the olive oil. Then add the celery, green pepper, sugar, canned tomatoes, tomato paste, some oregano, and chopped parsley. Let simmer for 1 hour, stirring as needed.

Preheat the oven to 350°. In a large pan, layer the tomato mixture, lasagna noodles, ricotta, Mozzarella, some Parmesan, and then the chopped spinach and tomatoes. Put the sauce on top. Sprinkle Parmesan on top. Bake for 1 hour.

Let stand for 10 minutes for better cutting and serving. Sprinkle the chopped fresh tomatoes on the very top. Sprinkle lightly with oregano, basil, and thyme, and then sprinkle Parmesan over all.

Serves 8

Judith Murray, Toronto, Ontario

Edie with Canadian friends

Chicken Fried Pork Chops

6	pork chops, about 3/4-inch thickness
2	eggs, beaten
2	tablespoons milk
1	cup fine cracker crumbs
1/4	cup fat
1/2	teaspoon salt
	Dash pepper
1/4	cup water

Pound the chops thoroughly with a meat pounder to 1/2-inch thickness. In a medium bowl, mix the eggs and milk. Dip the chops first into the egg mixture, then into the crumbs. In a skillet, heat the fat and brown the chops on both sides. Season with salt and pepper. Add water, cover, and cook over low heat for 45 to 60 minutes. Lift the chops occasionally to prevent sticking. For a crisp coating, remove the cover for the last 15 minutes.

Serves 6

Edie Hand

Great Pork Chop Skillet Dinner

6	lean pork chops
1/2	teaspoon salt
1/4	teaspoon pepper
1	tablespoon cooking oil
1/2	teaspoon Savory bay leaves
1/2	bay leaf
2	cups tomato juice
1/2	cup water
1	small cabbage, cut into 6 wedges
6	carrots, cut into 1-inch pieces (about 2 cups)
1 1/2	cups onion, coarsely chopped
3	medium potatoes, pared and quartered
1/4	teaspoon salt

Season the chops with the salt and pepper. In a large skillet, heat the oil and brown the chops. Add the bay leaves, tomato juice, and water. Cover and simmer for 30 minutes. Add the cabbage, carrots, onion, potatoes, and salt. Cover and simmer for 35 minutes or until the vegetables are tender.

Serves 6

Alice Hood Hacker,
grandmother of Edie Hand

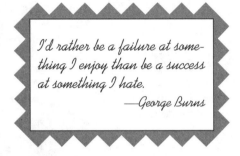

I'd rather be a failure at something I enjoy than be a success at something I hate.
—George Burns

Homestyle Ham Bake

1 1/2	pounds ham, ground
1 1/2	pounds fresh pork, ground
1 1/2	cups bread crumbs
2	eggs
1 1/4	cups milk
1	tablespoon prepared mustard
1	cup firmly packed brown sugar
1/4	cup cider vinegar
1/4	cup water

Preheat the oven to 350°. In a large mixing bowl, combine the ham, pork, bread crumbs, eggs, and milk. Form the mixture into a loaf and place in a 5" x 9" inch loaf pan. Bake for 45 minutes.

In a saucepan, combine the brown sugar, mustard, vinegar, and water. Boil the sauce ingredients for 5 minutes, or until thick. Pour over the loaf and bake for an additional 45 minutes or longer.

Serves 6

Edie Hand

Country Chicken with Bacon

4   boned chicken breasts
1   pound bacon
8   ounces sour cream
1   10³/₄-ounce can Cream
    of Mushroom soup
    Pinch pepper

Preheat the oven to 300°. Roll the chicken breasts and place 1 or 2 strips of bacon over each one. Place the breasts in a casserole dish. In a separate bowl, mix together the sour cream and Cream of Mushroom soup. Pepper the chicken breasts and pour the sour cream and soup mixture over them. Bake uncovered for 3 hours.

Serves 4

Edie Hand

Fricasseed Chicken Italian Style

2¹/₂ pounds chicken
¹/₄ cup seasoned flour
3   tablespoons vegetable
     oil
1   teaspoon rosemary
1   teaspoon garlic
2   tablespoons olive oil
¹/₃ cup wine vinegar

Dredge the chicken pieces in the flour. In a large skillet, heat the oil and brown the chicken. Discard the oil and wipe the skillet clean. Mix the rosemary and garlic. Heat the olive oil and return the chicken to the pan. Add the rosemary and garlic. Add the vinegar, cover, and cook on low for 45 minutes to 1 hour. If it cooks dry, add a little water.

Serves 4 to 6

Charles Mooney, London, England

Lively Lobster Creole

2   lobsters to a pot
3-4 quarts water
1   tablespoon salt per
    quart water

Bring the water to a boil and add the salt. Grasp each live lobster, one at a time, by cupping your hand around the back and plunging it headfirst into the boiling water. Cover the pot and after the water returns to a boil, cook for 5 to 6 minutes per pound. Test for doneness. Pull on an antenna on the head. If it comes out easily, it is done. Drain the lobsters and serve hot.

Variation: For steamed lobster, pour 1 inch of water into a large kettle and bring to a boil over high heat. Add the lobsters, cover, and steam for 15 minutes.

Stacie Benes, Washington, D.C.

Sensational and Savory Stew

1	tablespoon oil	1	15-ounce can sliced potatoes
½	cup onion, chopped	1	10¾-ounce can Cream of Celery soup
½	cup celery, chopped		
½	cup green pepper, chopped	1	10¾-ounce can Cream of Chicken soup
4	chicken breasts, cooked and cubed		
1	14½-ounce can tomato chunks	1	16-ounce can pork 'n beans
		1	11-ounce can kernel corn
1	10-ounce can diced Ro-tel tomatoes	1	15-ounce can lima beans
		½	package Southwestern herb mix
1	8-ounce can tomato sauce		Salt and pepper to taste

In a large pot, heat the oil and sauté the onion, celery, and green pepper. Add the remaining ingredients and cook for 15 to 20 minutes.

Edie Hand

Bama Beef and Rice

1	pound ground beef
2	tablespoons butter
1	medium onion, diced
1	medium green pepper, chopped
½	cup converted rice
1	teaspoon salt
¼	teaspoon pepper
1	6-ounce can tomato juice
2	cups hot water

Preheat the oven to 350°. In a heavy 10" skillet, cook the beef just until it loses its redness. Crumble the meat with a fork and place it in a buttered casserole dish. In a separate skillet, melt 1 tablespoon of the butter and cook the onion and green pepper until wilted. Add the vegetables to the beef. In the same skillet, cook the rice in the remaining butter, stirring constantly until golden. Add the rice to the beef and season with salt and pepper. Stir together the tomato paste and water to blend. Pour over the beef mixture. Do not stir. Bake about 1 hour until the rice is tender. The tomato mixture will be on top.

Serves 6

Marsha Kinsaul, Dora, Alabama

Edie cooking up tunes with cousin
Donna Presley Early

The Best "During Church" Beef Roast or Tenderloin

Heat oven to 500°. Rub your favorite seasonings (I think you *must* include garlic) over your tenderloin or any lean, tender cut of beef. Place in shallow roasting pan and do not cover. Cook for 5 minutes per pound for rare; 6 minutes per pound for medium rare; and 7 minutes per pound for done. Turn off the oven. Do not open the oven door. Leave undisturbed for 2 hours.

Come home from church and enjoy.

Judy Spencer Nelon, Brentwood, Tennessee

David's Spicy Chili

1½ pounds ground sirloin
1   large onion, chopped
¾   large (14 ounces) can tomato sauce
1   14.8-ounce can diced tomatoes
1   10-ounce can Ro-tel tomatoes
1   small can chopped green chilies

1   16-ounce can dark red kidney beans
2   16-ounce cans of hot chili beans
1   teaspoon chili powder
1   teaspoon Worcestershire sauce
¼   cup ketchup
½   can beer

Brown the ground sirloin and chopped onions. Drain grease. Mix rest of ingredients and simmer for about 45 to 60 minutes.

David Hall, Nashville, Tennessee,
president, TNN, CBS

Chicken A-La Can Can

From the New York Times *Food Section:*
1   can Cream of Chicken soup
1   can Cream of Mushroom soup
1   can instant rice
1   can water
1   can baked and boned chicken
1   can prepared onion rings

Mix all of the ingredients together in a saucepan and simmer on the stove until the mixture boils, then remove from the stove, place onion rings on the top, and bake in the oven at 350° for 30 minutes.

Dr. Marlene Reed, Leeds, Alabama

Grandma's Penicillin—Greek Lemon Chicken Orzo Soup

1½ cups orzo
¼   cup fresh lemon juice
2   tablespoons chicken
    soup base
2   quarts water
2   cups chicken, cooked
    and shredded
¼   cup fresh lemon juice
2   cans Cream of Chicken
    soup

Cook orzo and drain and rinse. Mix chicken soup base in 2 quarts water. Add chicken and lemon juice. Gently fold in orzo. Just before serving add lemon juice. Heat through, but do not boil. Season to taste.

Makes 3 quarts

Nancy D. Gross, Gadsden, Alabama

Spicy Grilled Chicken—Definitely "Finger-Lickin' Good"

Lots of chicken—4 legs,
    4 thighs, 4 wings,
    4 breasts
1   16-ounce Kraft Zesty
    Italian fat free dressing
1   cup barbeque sauce
    (your choice of flavor)
½   cup of Dale's Steak
    Sauce
¼   cup Worcestershire
    sauce
¼   cup Bishop's 3-in-1
    barbeque sauce (can be
    more of less depending
    on how hot and spicy
    you want your chicken
    . . . if unavailable in
    your area, use hot
    sauce)

Preparation of chickens (chicken should be rinsed before using): Slice into the thickest portions of the legs, thighs, and breasts 2 to 3 times. This aids in the cooking process and exposes more chicken to the sauce.

Mix the above ingredients into a 4-quart mixing bowl.

Add one piece of chicken at a time to the sauce. Carefully mixing the chicken and sauce together. Fill the rest of the bowl with chicken, cover, and allow to marinate at room temperature for 2 hours.

Grill chicken on low to medium heat. The key to grilled chicken is cooking it slowly and turning it often. Save the sauce that you used to marinate the chicken to baste the chicken as you turn when it appears to be getting dry. Once you start basting the chicken, baste each time you turn. Remember—cook slowly with a lot of turns.

Cook until done. Enjoy!

Mark Aldridge, Athens, Alabama

Poor Man's Supper

1	pound ground beef
1	medium onion, cut up
1	small can tomato sauce
1	small bell pepper, cut up
2	cups leftover cooked pinto beans
1	recipe of your corn bread mixture

Brown ground beef in skillet and, when nearly done, add the onions, tomato sauce, and bell pepper. Cook this for about 8 to 10 minutes. In a greased loaf pan or large skillet, add the ground beef mixture. Then add 2 cups cold (leftover cooked) pinto beans on top of that. Then add your corn bread mixture (made just like you usually make your corn bread) on top of that and bake in your preheated oven at 350° for about 40 to 45 minutes or until corn bread is done. This is a meal in one pan—your meat, beans, and bread.

Good meal in cold weather time.

Dorothy Gober, Burnout, Alabama,
Edie's childhood friend

One-Pot Chop 'n Hot

	Black-eyed peas (I use Trappey's brand)
4-6	smoked pork chops
2	15-ounce or 16-ounce cans jalapeño peppers

In medium to large pot, put the 2 cans of black-eyed peas. Be sure to include the liquid in the cans. On the top of the peas, place the smoked pork chops (these chops are already cooked and can be found pre-wrapped in your grocer's meat department). Bring to a gentle boil; reduce heat and simmer for 30 minutes or more (the longer the simmer, the better the taste). Top with jalapeño peppers.

This is an easy recipe to double or triple for a crowd.

I serve rice, cole slaw, and homemade cornbread with this dish.

Yields 2 "healthy" or 4 "skimpy" servings

Norma Simpson, Spanish Fort, Alabama

Bonnie's Lasagna

My dad's favorite meal is steak (rare) and baked potato. However, he also likes Italian food and when he's home for any length of time I'll fix lasagna or spaghetti. His favorite way to eat spaghetti is with butter and salt and pepper—no sauce. He usually has a first helping with sauce and calls his second helping with butter his dessert. Following is my recipe for lasagna.

1   large box of lasagna noodles
2   cans Hunts traditional spaghetti sauce
1   large bag of shredded Mozzarella cheese
1   large tub of cottage cheese
    Parmesan cheese
1   large (2-pound) package ground chuck

Cook noodles according to directions. Brown hamburger, drain fat off, pour sauce into pan with meat, and stir.

Layer lasagna:
    Sauce
    Noodles
    Cottage cheese
    Shredded cheese (sprinkle a little over cottage cheese)
    Sprinkle Parmesan cheese
    Noodles
    Sauce
    Noodles
    Sauce
    Remaining shredded Mozzarella cheese
    Parmesan cheese
    Bake at 350° for 30 minutes. Serve with salad and garlic bread.

Bonnie Allison-Farr, Hueytown, Alabama,
daughter of Nascar race driver Bobby Allison

Chicken and Dressing

Cook chicken in butter, onions, and celery until it falls off bone. Save broth to use in dressing.

Cook cornbread. In large mixing bowl, crumble cornbread and 3 or 4 wet slices of loafbread and celery and onions from broth. Add 12 cut-up boiled eggs. Use either broth or combinations of the following soups: Cream of Chicken, Cream of Celery, or Cream of Mushroom soup. Add teaspoon of sage, teaspoon of pepper, and teaspoon of salt or poultry seasoning. Add 3 or 4 drops of hot sauce. Add enough water to make soupy for moist dressing. Taste. Add 3 raw eggs. Pour in 2 greased casserole dishes and bake at 350° for 1 hour. Delicious! Can save 1 casserole dish for cooking later—you will have a demand for it!

Kay Parker, Florence, Alabama,
counselor at the Northwest Alabama Cancer Center

Old-Timey Vegetable Soup

2	beef bouillon cubes
1	bunch carrots
1	head of cauliflower
2	onions
4	cloves garlic
2	bay leaves
2	cans crushed tomatoes
1	bunch celery
1	head of broccoli
6	potatoes
½	teaspoons liquid hot sauce

Delicious, nutritious, and feeds 8 to 10 people. Fat free.

Easy to do: Boil bouillon cubes in about a quart of water until dissolved. Pour into very large pot. Add tomatoes. Chop all vegetables into bitesize pieces. Add to pot (firmer veggies first). Add more water...

Enough to cover all veggies. Let simmer until the vegetables are still a little firm, but done. Season to taste. Freeze leftovers in small, individual freezer bags. Makes a great meal next week, too.

Roy Clark, Tulsa, Oklahoma,
Internationally renowned guitarist/country western
singer/host of Hee Haw

Me and Roy Clark backstage at the University of North Alabama, 1992

Edie and Annie (alias "Nurse Lyla") rehearsing on As the World Turns set

Curried Chicken

Ingredients:

1	2-3 pound chicken
1/4	cup butter or margarine
1	medium sized onion
1	tablespoon curry powder
1/4	cup flour
1	teaspoon salt
1	cup chicken broth and a bit of milk
	Rice

Toppings:

Raisins
Toasted coconut
Toasted peanuts
Tomatoes
Bananas
Chunk pineapple
Olives
Etc.

Boil chicken until it comes off bone (about 45 minutes to 1 hour). Let cool and separate from bone.

Sauce may be prepared in double boiler or regular skillet. Melt butter in pan and add chopped onion. Cook slowly on medium heat about 10 to 15 minutes or until onion is slightly brown. Mix curry powder with flour. Add to butter and onions. Have milk and chicken broth ready and add after flour is added. Add salt. Let it thicken. This takes about 2 to 3 minutes. Add chicken. It's done.

Serve the chicken mixture on rice. Add toppings as desired.

Marline Sellers, Florence, Alabama,
University of North Alabama and Zeta Tau Alpha Fraternity alumnae

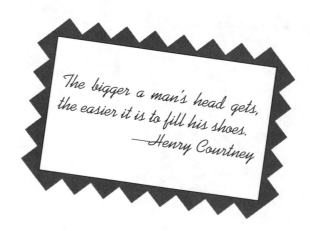

The bigger a man's head gets, the easier it is to fill his shoes.
—Henry Courtney

Meatballs

1   pound of ground beef
     or chuck
2   eggs
     Bread crumbs
     Garlic salt
     Romano cheese
     Chopped onion
Sauce:
1   29-ounce can Hunt's
     tomato puree
1   29-ounce can Hunt's
     tomato sauce
1   12-ounce can tomato
     paste

Combine first 6 ingredients and roll into balls. Place in oven and bake at 350° until brown on both sides. Add sauce.

Sauce: Brown 1 pound of ground beef and drain. Add Hunt's tomato puree, Hunt's tomato sauce, and tomato paste. Add a dash of garlic salt to taste. Dash whole basil leaves over the sauce and add 1½ shakes of oregano, 1 tablespoon sugar, and 1 shot of whiskey. Cook 3 hours on low heat and serve with the meatballs.

Sue Blackburn Hardesty, Highland, Indiana,
Edie's Mom

Sue's Beef Brisket

1   whole trimmed beef
     brisket
½   cup soy sauce
½   cup liquid smoke
½   cup Worcestershire
     sauce
     Black pepper
1   medium or large onion,
     quartered

Place brisket in large foil-lined pan. Mix soy sauce, liquid smoke, and Worcestershire, and pour over brisket. Pepper to taste and put onions on top. Put another piece of foil over top and seal tightly. Making sure no juice escapes into pan.

Cook at 300° and all day or at least 5 hours. Cool for 30 minutes. Slice on angle.

Sue Dodge, Vienna, Virginia,
Southern gospel singer who appears on
Gaither Homecomings, TNN

Flip-Flop Pork Chops

You just baste them with flour salt and pepper. Cook in an electric skillet or regular skillet until brown. Bring 1 can of mushroom soup to a boil with one can of water. Pour over the pork chops and steam for 5 to 15 minutes.

Sue Blackburn Hardesty, Highland, Indiana,
Edie's Mom

Gourmet

Venison Turrine

Meaty bones (neck,
ribs, etc.) from one deer
1   pack unflavored gelatin
for every 2 cups meat
1   tablespoon salt
1/2 teaspoon black pepper
1/4 teaspoon red pepper
5   cloves garlic, minced
2   medium yellow onions
Bay leaves, parsley,
rosemary, and tarragon
tied together in a
bouquet garnish
2   cups cranberry juice
2   cups dry sherry

Boil all together in large pot with enough water to cover. Add water as necessary, and simmer until meat can easily be removed from bones. Remove bones, and coarse chop meat into separate large bowl. Continue in batches until all meat has been done, adding water as needed. Reduce broth to 1/3, adjust seasoning if necessary.

For each 2 cups meat, you will need one package unflavored gelatin. Wet gelatin by sprinkling over 1/4 cup per package with cool water in a small bowl. Add 1/4 cup (for each 2 cups meat) reduced stock to gelatin and stir until dissolved. Add to meat only enough of the gelatin mixture to thoroughly moisten meat, mixing well. Press firmly into loaf pans. Chill until solid. Dip loaf pan in hot water for a few moments and unmold. Slice thinly and serve cold, as on a sandwich. Extra broth makes great soup or chili base.

Roland Bramblette, Jasper, Alabama

Fettuccini Alfredo

1   12-ounce package
Creamette Folded Egg
Fettuccini
1/4 pound soft butter
1/4 cup whipping cream,
room temperature
1   egg yolk, slightly
beaten
3/4 cup Parmesan cheese,
freshly grated
White pepper to taste

Prepare Creamette Folded Egg Fettuccini according to package directions. Drain. In same large pan that fettuccini was cooked in, add butter and toss with fettuccini. Combine cream and egg yolk. Alternate 1/3 the cream and 1/3 the cheese; tossing well, but gently after each addition. Add pepper to taste. Serve immediately.

6 servings

Edie Hand

Tomatoes Stuffed with Vermicelli Pesto

25   medium tomatoes
1½   pounds vermicelli
½   cup pesto
     Sweet basil leaves

Hollow out the tomatoes by cutting off the stem with a sharp serrated knife and removing the seeds with a melon scoop. Turn the tomatoes upside down on a rack to drain before filling with pasta.

Cook vermicelli according to package, drain.

Pesto:

½   cup pignolia nuts (pine nuts)
4   cloves garlic, peeled
1   teaspoon salt
½   teaspoon freshly ground pepper
3   cups fresh basil leaves
¼   pound Parmesan cheese, freshly grated
¼   pound Romano cheese, freshly grated
1½ cups olive oil

In the food processor, grind all ingredients until fine with ½ cup olive oil, add remaining oil until smooth and creamy.

Variation: Walnuts, parsley, or spinach may be added.

Mix vermicelli with pesto. Fill the tomatoes with the pasta and top each with 1 or 2 basil leaves.

Edie Hand

Jack Voorhies, alias "Paw," and Edie, alias "Pearl," in a national commercial

Edie

Shrimphony

This dish is inspired by a musical symphony, which is why it is named "shrimphony." The name implies that it is a combination of magical ingredients, each providing its unique "note" and making a unique contribution to the whole. While making this dish, think of an entire orchestra accompanying you in your creation. Then savor each bite, appreciating the individual contributions, as well as the enchantment they create when combined.

The metaphor of a symphony in this dish also applies to all of your life, as you combine different roles (lover, worker, parent, friend, believer, playmate), feelings, relationships, and activities, to make up the totality of your being. As a psychologist, talk radio advice host, TV personality, lecturer, and author, I strive each day to integrate all these jobs in a magical orchestration. And as a bass guitarist, I thank my friend, New York bass guitarist Matt Feinberg, for this recipe that brought me back into loving cooking, and adding that ingredient to the symphony of my life.

Based on service for two, you will need:

1	pound jumbo shrimp	4	cups jasmine rice

Sauce:
- 1/4 cup apricot preserves
- 1/2 cup pineapple chutney
- 1/2 cup teriyaki sauce
- 1/8 cup honey mustard
- 3 tablespoons ginger, grated
- Old Bay Seasoning to taste
- Vinegar to taste
- Olive oil
- 4 cloves garlic, chopped
- Chopped red pepper
- 1/2 8-ounce can of water chestnuts boiled in water
- 1/2 15-ounce can of straw mushrooms
- 1/2 can baby corn
- 1 cup orange juice
- 2 slices chopped or crushed fresh pineapple

Mix to make a marinade: apricots, chutney, teriyaki sauce, honey mustard, grated ginger. Boil shrimp until barely done (undercook a little) in Old Bay Seasoning and vinegar. Peel shrimp and marinate in prepared sauce for 1/2 hour. Make jasmine rice. In cast iron frying pan, put enough olive oil to cover pan. Take shrimp out of marinade and put in pan, adding garlic and chopped red pepper. Fry for 2 minutes until red (do not overcook). Drain excess oil from frying pan and add marinade. Add remaining ingredients, then pass pan under the broiler in the oven (2 minutes or until sauce thickens). Pour over jasmine rice and serve.

Dr. Judy Kuriansky, New York, New York,
author and national radio talk show host

Marsha Folsom's Attitude for Life

To make life sweet, you have to stir it up a little.

∾

The words above describe, in a nutshell, the positive attitude that Alabama's former first lady, Marsha Folsom, possesses to the fullest. Those words were passed down through lessons that Marsha learned through her grandmother. Little did she know at the time that those words would transform into the legacy that comprises her attitude for life.

Marsha remembers vividly the spectacular taste of her grandmother's iced tea. She says, "My grandmother was a minister's wife and a wonderful cook. She made the best iced tea! She would let it steep just right, and she made syrup with hot water and sugar that she would add to the tea to sweeten it. I remember asking her why her tea tasted so good and she told me that it wasn't because of the sugar she added, but rather because of all the stirring she did. I learned a lesson from that comment. Life is like that because if you want life to be sweet, then you have to stir it. You have to stir things up in life, persevere, and get involved. You also have to be aware of who's there for you in different stages of your life as you grow and flourish, and look at those people as blessings."

Marsha's father is one of those blessings. A farmer and a cotton ginner in rural Cullman County, Alabama, he was also the owner of a country store. Marsha says that the store was the "hub" of their little community.

She remembers, "My father was a merchant, but he also believed that it was his mission to help that community to grow and prosper. Farming teaches you to live on faith, and from that, as well as in his career in politics, my father learned at an early age that times can be rough and that people don't always treat you with respect. He has been an inspiration to me because no matter what, he finds a way and has faith in God, himself, and the gifts he has been given."

Marsha says that through her father she learned the importance of listening and caring about people. She notes that listening is an important tool when you are a public servant, and her listening skills only add to her zest for life—the important thing about listening is that you must listen also with your heart.

"You do the right thing when you listen with your heart. Through the life my family lived, they provided an illustration to

friends

me from a young age that one should help others. With this and what I have been blessed with, I see that God is my strength, and I am so thankful for the vigor and zest that He has instilled in me and the people that have come through my life and been there. I know they have been there for a reason. It is through my spiritual strength that I have recognized the values in my life like love and strength. It's been illustrated to me that to whom much is given, much is expected. If I had to describe my attitude for life in one word, it would be zest. When I think of the word zest, I think of energy and enthusiasm. I also think of it as a spice. I tend to look at the world in a positive sense, but there's something about spice that adds flavor and texture to not only food, but life."

Marsha's zest for life not only spices up her life, but the lives of all she comes in contact with. If it's true that to make life sweet you have to stir it up a little, then Marsha's life is one of the sweetest of them all. She has not only stirred life to the brim, but she has enjoyed it along the way.

The former governor and first lady of
Alabama Jim and Marsha Folsom

friends

Shrimp Miriliton

5	mirilitons
1	stick butter
2	pounds small peeled shrimp
1	cup onion, chopped
2	garlic cloves, chopped
2	bay leaves
1	tablespoon parsley, chopped
1	teaspoon salt
1/4	teaspoon pepper
1	tablespoon Worcestershire sauce
1/4	teaspoon Tabasco
3/4	cup Italian bread crumbs

Boil whole miriliton until pierces easily with fork (45 minutes). Peel skin, remove seeds and center strings; mash pulp. Melt butter, add shrimp and pulp, onions, garlic, bay leaves, and parsley, and simmer over low heat 20 minutes, stirring to keep from sticking. Add salt, pepper, Worcestershire, and Tabasco. Simmer 5 minutes—add bread crumbs slowly to absorb moisture. Cook another 5 minutes, stirring. Remove bay leafs—spread buttered crumbs over casserole. Bake uncovered at 375°.

M. J. Myers, New York, New York

Crab & Corn Bisque

1/2	pound butter
3	tablespoons flour
1	large onion, chopped
1	quart milk
1	16-ounce can cream style corn
1	can Cream of Potato soup
1/4	teaspoon mace
1/4	teaspoon red pepper
1	pint picked crabmeat
1/4	pound Swiss cheese, grated
2	tablespoons parsley, snipped
2	tablespoons green onions, finely chopped

In large heavy pot, melt butter. Stir in flour until well blended, but not brown; add onions. Cook on medium heat until onions are soft—about 10 minutes. Add all but last four ingredients. Simmer about 15 minutes—be careful not to scorch. Before serving, stir in crabmeat, cheese, parsley, and green onions.

Note: This is to die for! Take a taste, close your eyes, and you very well may hear "dah saints go marchin' in."

Serves 6 to 8 elegantly

Marsha Folsom, Cullman, Alabama, wife of former Alabama Governor Jim Folsom Jr.

Three-Cheese Lasagna

Meals are very special—a great time to spend with loved ones (family or friends) and forget about troubles and circumstances that may be unpleasant. I enjoy preparing foods because I know I am providing an enjoyable time for my family— it is so rewarding to see them healthy and physically developing into special people.

This lasagna is a shortened version of a food we enjoy in our home without the fuss and time that it takes to make lasagna with cooked noodles. This dish is very spicy with basil, oregano, and garlic, and a treat!

1	pound ground chuck
1	small onion, chopped, or 1 tablespoon dehydrated onions
2	teaspoons dried basil
1	teaspoon dried oregano
2	garlic cloves, minced
4	cups canned or prepared spaghetti sauce
1	15-ounce can peeled tomatoes
4	eggs, beaten
12	ounces low fat cottage cheese
½	teaspoon dried basil
1	8-ounce box (uncooked) lasagna noodles
1	pound Mozzarella cheese slices
2	cups Mild Cheddar cheese, grated Parmesan cheese, grated

Brown ground chunk in heavy skillet. Drain excess fat. Add onions, basil, oregano, and garlic. Mix well. Add spaghetti sauce and chopped peeled tomatoes. Simmer for 30 minutes.

While spaghetti sauce is cooking, beat eggs well. Then add cottage cheese and basil to eggs. Set aside.

Preheat oven to 350°.

In a 13" x 9" x 3" Pyrex or lasagna pan, add a layer of spaghetti sauce, then add layer of uncooked lasagna noodles.

Layer half of egg mixture. Cover with ½ pound of Mozzarella cheese slices. Then sprinkle layer with grated Cheddar cheese. Then sprinkle with grated Parmesan cheese. Repeat the "layering" steps. Cover lasagna with remaining spaghetti sauce. Place in oven for 45 to 60 minutes. Remove from oven and sprinkle with grated Parmesan cheese. Allow to cool for 10 to 15 minutes before cutting into portions.

Maria Brown Ephraim, Hoover, Alabama

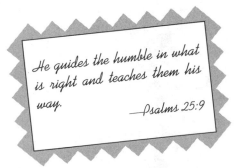

He guides the humble in what is right and teaches them his way.
—Psalms 25:9

Cuban Black Bean Soup

1	pound black beans
2	quarts water
2	tablespoons salt
5	cloves garlic, peeled
1/2	tablespoon cumin
1/2	tablespoon oregano
1	ounce white vinegar
5	ounces spanish oil
1/2	pound onions
1/2	pound green peppers

Soak beans in water overnight. Add salt, boil beans until soft. Crush in a mortar the garlic, cumin, oregano, and vinegar. Heat the oil in a pan, adding the onions and peppers, cut in very small pieces, and fry until the onions are brown. Add crushed ingredients, frying slowly. Drain some of the water off the beans before adding them to the pan and cook slowly until ready to serve. Boil a small portion of rice and marinate it in finely chopped raw onions, Spanish oil, and vinegar. Add 1 soup spoon of this to each serving.

Serves 6

Betsy Bass, Florence, Alabama,
University of North Alabama Zeta Tau Alpha Alumnae

For further study on the topic of humility, go to the Naves Topical Bible search on humility at www.goshen.net.

Heart Healthy

Shrimp Gumbo

2   cups fresh okra, sliced, or 1 10-ounce package frozen no-salt-added okra, sliced

¼   cup acceptable vegetable oil

⅔   cup green onions and tops, chopped

3   cloves garlic, finely chopped

½   teaspoon freshly ground black pepper, or to taste

2   cups water

1   cup canned no-salt-added tomatoes

2   whole bay leaves

½   cup uncooked rice

1   pound fresh medium shrimp, peeled and deveined

6   drops hot pepper sauce

In a large stockpot, over medium-high heat, sauté okra in oil for 10 minutes. Add onions, garlic, and pepper. Cook about 5 minutes. Add water, tomatoes and bay leaves. Cover and simmer 20 minutes.

Meanwhile, cook rice according to package directions; do not use salt, butter, or margarine. Set aside.

Add shrimp to okra mixture. Cover and remove from heat. Let stand 5 minutes, or until shrimp is done (when it turns pink). Do not overcook.

Remove bay leaves and sprinkle in hot pepper sauce. Stir to mix well.

Place ¼ cup of cooked rice in each soup bowl. Add equal amounts of gumbo to each bowl and serve hot.

Serves 6; ¾ cup per serving

a favorite of Edie Hand
as found in American Heart Association Cookbook:
5th Edition

We are what we repeatedly do. Excellence, then, is not an act, but a habit.

—Aristotle

Delicious Crab Cakes

1 pound cooked crab meat or 2 6-ounce cans crab meat, drained and rinsed	1 tablespoon fresh lemon juice
	1 cup fresh breadcrumbs, grated
2 egg whites, lightly beaten	2 teaspoons minced fresh dill or 1 teaspoon dried dill
1¼ cups sour cream (reduced-calorie if desired)	1 lemon, cut into wedges for garnish
1 cup green onions, chopped	Parsley for garnish

In large bowl, blend crab, egg whites, ¼ sour cream, ½ cup green onions, and lemon juice. Form mixture into 1" diameter patties. Combine bread crumbs and dill. Roll cakes in crumb mixture. Place on large baking sheet and bake in preheated 375° oven 10 to 15 minutes. In small bowl, combine remaining sour cream and green onions. Serve cakes garnished with lemon wedges and parsley and pass the sour cream mixture to accent cakes.

Lou Schefano, Graysville, Alabama

Dave's Special Eggs: Made for Special People!

It's kind of a "south of the Border" take on scrambled eggs but very enjoyable to prepare, and easy, too.

Scramble up some eggs with green onions, ripe avocado, diced Roma tomatoes, fresh cilantro, jack cheese, sliced zucchini, and any other vegetable you prefer. Then at the last moment, crumble up a healthy amount of blue corn tortilla chips into the eggs and stir up. Meanwhile, heat up a can of refried black beans in a saucepan and prepare your fajita style flour torillas, by buttering them up and heating them in a frying pan until golden brown. When all the items are prepared and ready, it is time to make your "special egg fajita." Take a tortilla, place some of the refried beans in it then put a healthy helping of eggs on top. Then top it off with some fresh salsa and roll up. Enjoy! I have made this recipe many times and have only heard *quebueno* after serving!

Dave Koz, Beverly Hills, California,
famous jazz saxophone artist and national radio host for Dave Koz Show

Heart Healthy Breakfast

1 cup Quaker Regular Oatmeal   2 cups water
Pinch of salt

Cook oatmeal nice and slow, until creamy. This takes only a few minutes. Put finished cereal into 2 bowls.

Top with: 1 banana, split between the 2 bowls, 1 handful each toasted sliced almonds, and 1 handful each raisins. In season, skip raisins and add fresh peaches, strawberries or raspberries. Serve with a piece of whole wheat toast on the side.

Jim Riley, Birmingham, Alabama,
president, Hindsight Management, Inc.

Dave Koz's Attitude for Life

Listen to your inner voice and trust your gut.

❧

Imagine the feeling of standing on stage and having thousands of people cheer for you and long for every moment that you can entertain them with your gift. Imagine possessing the gift of music and a heart for others, all while maintaining a low-key and humble attitude. Think about how it would feel to have your very own Web site that people visit just because they admire you.

Now, picture this dream becoming a reality, not just because of hard work, but because you followed the words above. You listened to that inner voice, trusted your gut, and now you are reaping the benefits. It may sound impossible, but for one man, this dream world is nothing but a blessed reality.

The advice above stems from one of the most talented musicians within the industry. Dave Koz has entertained audiences for years and is still continuing to spread his gift through his saxophone work. He hosts *The Dave Koz Radio Show* and his version of "Faces of the Heart" was used on *General Hospital.* He not only shares the words above with others, but those words have combined to add to his vivid recipe for life.

Dave says, "The main thing that comes back over and over is to listen to that inner voice and trust your gut because there has been a constant battle in my life of mind over gut. I have let my mind win a lot and that has taken me away from what I am to do. Whatever it is that you are to give to others, just listen to yourself and be your own person. That is what is right."

Many people may struggle through life not knowing exactly what is right and what is wrong, but Dave learned this at an early age as a result of being blessed with a family strong in ethics and values. His family is not only the heart of his conscience, but the heart of his inspiration. The road he traveled with his family was not always pleasant, and had several obstacles along the way. Dave knew early on that his mission in life was music and he had to work hard to overcome these obstacles and achieve his goal.

According to Dave, "One of the most inspiring things that has happened in my life is the fact that I have grown up with a good family ethic. My family was very supportive of my brothers and me

friends

and also our dreams. I lost my dad two years ago and I was very close to him. Strangely enough, my dad is as much a part of my life now in his absence physically from my life as when he was here in body. He has definitely been here and I think in a big way helped me to get where I am, not by pulling strings, but to keep me on track and keep me growing as a human being. One of my dreams and missions in life is music. Music is one of the more obvious ways that I am supposed to do what it is that I am supposed to do. It makes me happy and it is one of the things that drives me. People respond to the music in a powerful way and that keeps me going more than anything else. I think that all aspects of my career, my public career, not only exist to give me something to do, but also to increase the texture of other people's lives. Then, when I feel that what I am doing is doing that, I think everyone wins. And then I feel good in much the same way that I look to movies, art exhibits, or somebody's poems to enrich my life."

The music industry is a tough one to tackle, especially alone. Fortunately for Dave, he has always had support and been filled with special opportunities that have facilitated his dream.

He says, "I have led a very blessed kind of life and I didn't have to struggle that much. A lot of people struggle with their careers and they either never make it or it takes a very long time. I was

Dave and Edie at the 1998 Smooth Jazz Christmas Special in Atlanta, Georgie. Dave's latest CD's are December Makes Me Feel This Way *and* The Dance, *on Capitol Records*

friends

signed to a record deal after my first demo. It sort of fell in my lap and I just don't ever want to take that for granted. I have worked a lot and paid my dues in other ways and I feel that I can use my music to say what I am feeling inside. I let my heart lead the way and I love to feast on different things of knowledge. I strive to be a compassionate person and I want to feel what other people feel and to walk in other people's shoes. That makes me a better person."

One way that Dave interacts with people and listens to them is through his own chat page at www.davekoz.com. He said, "Thirty or forty people have met through my chat page, and they come together to concerts and have done a lot of things for my charities. For two years in a row they have gathered funds among themselves and presented me with checks for thousands of dollars to the Starlight Children's Foundation that grants wishes to seriously ill children and also to the American Heart Association in honor of my dad, who died of a heart attack. They have created all of this good and love and they always get together for my birthday and that blows me away. The power of people coming together and the fact that I could help them blows me away."

Dave may get blown away by his fans, but that is small in comparison to those that are blown away by his compassion and talent. He has appeared on *General Hospital* and *Melrose Place,* and he was showcased during "Quincy Jones: The First 50 Years" and on the Disney Channel's 1998 American Teacher Awards.

He has recently released a new CD, *The Dance.* Dave is charting his own course and is more relaxed and focused than ever before. This is partly owing to the fact that Dave not only gives the advice that makes up his recipe for life, but he follows it. Imagine the power that comes from succeeding at your dream. Dave knows that power and he shares his gift with others. He does not have to imagine changing lives, because he already does it. If your inner voice is speaking to you, don't hesitate to follow it. Just imagine. Your dream is only a chance away. Just ask Dave.

friends

friends

With all of life's ups and downs, God should be the first and foremost ingredient in anyone's recipe for life. Take a good blend of family values with a huge helping of life in order to guarantee a prosperous life. If you're not careful, bitterness can seep in on your fine mixture and spoil life's batter. Just remember to sprinkle a little goodness around there and the sweetness, I promise, will come right on through!

—Kathy L. Hope, Ft. Payne, Alabama,
cousin of Randy Owen of the group Alabama

my partner in environmental causes, Randy
Owen of the group Alabama

Side Dishes

Hominy and Corn Casserole

3   15½-ounce cans white hominy, drained

2   11-ounce cans white corn, drained

1   4-ounce can chopped green chiles, drained

1   tablespoon cornstarch

½   teaspoon ground white pepper

¼   teaspoon salt

1   8-ounce container sour cream

1½ cups (6 ounces) Monterey Jack cheese, shredded

1½ cups (6 ounces) processed American cheese, shredded
    Paprika

Rinse hominy and drain well. Combine hominy and next 6 ingredients. Spoon half of hominy mixture into a lightly greased 11" x 7" baking dish. Combine shredded cheeses; sprinkle half of cheese over casserole. Spoon remaining hominy mixture over cheese. Bake, covered, at 350 degrees for 35 minutes or until thoroughly heated. Sprinkle casserole with remaining cheese and paprika, and bake, uncovered, 5 minutes.

Makes 10 to 12 servings

Mrs. Gerald Goode, Dora, Alabama

Rice Consommé

1¾ cups uncooked rice

2   cans beef consommé

1   stick butter

Grease baking dish. Pour in rice. Pour in cans of liquid. Cut up stick of butter and place in mixture. Bake covered at 350°. Stir when butter melts. Cook until soup dissolves.

Billy Brown, photographer

Lee Ann and Billy baking up some delights!

Mouthwatering Macaroni and Cheese

2½ cups water
1 teaspoon salt
1 cup uncooked macaroni
¼ pound sharp Cheddar cheese
¼ pound mild Cheddar cheese
4 tablespoons margarine, melted
2 eggs, beaten
2 cups milk
¼ teaspoon salt

Bring water and 1 teaspoon salt to boil; add macaroni and cook until tender; drain and let cool. Put a layer of macaroni in a baking dish and cover with layer of cheese. Repeat. Pour margarine over the macaroni. Combine eggs, milk, and ¼ teaspoon salt; Pour over macaroni and bake at 350° for 30 minutes.

Angela Lockhart, Jasper, Alabama

Fried Green Tomatoes

¾ cup self-rising flour
¼ cup cornmeal
¼ teaspoon salt
¼ teaspoon pepper
¾ cup milk
3-4 green tomatoes, cut into ¼-inch slices
Vegetable oil

Combine first 5 ingredients; mix until smooth. Add additional milk to thin, if necessary; batter should resemble pancake batter. Working in batches, dip tomato slices into batter, allowing excess batter to drip back into bowl. Fry in 2" hot oil (375°) in a large heavy skillet until browned, turning once carefully with tongs. Transfer to a colander to drain.

Yield: 3 to 4 servings

Fannie Flagg
as seen in Fannie Flagg's
Original Whistle Stop Café Cookbook

"Pop" Soup (Avgolemono)

4 cans chicken stock
⅓ cup uncooked rice
6 eggs
6 tablespoons lemon juice
Dash salt
Dash pepper

Boil broth. Add rice and reduce heat. Cook about 15 minutes, partially uncovered. Lower heat. Beat eggs until frothy. Add lemon juice. Add, slowly, 1 cup of broth to egg, stirring constantly. Pour this into pot of broth and rice. Heat for 5 minutes. Do not boil. Salt and pepper to taste.

My grandfather added 2 egg whites and 1 tablespoon lemon and beat into a meringue and dalloped on top.

Serves 4

Tom Cherones, Florence, Oregon

Fannie Flagg's Attitude for Life

To have a calmer life is to live simpler.

❧

Fannie Flagg is a woman of distinction. Her attitude has enabled her to turn a dream of writing into a reality. She is a woman who has had good timing in her career, been persistent, and known how to position herself for success. Fannie has a passion for keeping memories alive through the stroke of her pen like in her best-selling novels, *Daisy Fay and the Miracle Man* and *Fried Green Tomatoes,* and in her new novel, *Welcome to the World Baby Girl.* They are all stories related to her childhood memories of people, places, and things, with a touch of her own unique flavor to bring those characters alive to entertain us all.

Fannie says she likes where she is during this stage in her life and is grateful to have a calmer, simpler lifestyle, even in the mist of all her continued success as a writer. She says, "My strength to keep on keepin' on comes from God and the fact I

Fellow Alabamian Fannie Flagg

fun

might make a difference in someone's life." Years ago, her sixth grade teacher in Foley, Alabama, Sybil Underwood, recognized something in her that no one else cared to see at that stage of her life. "I'll never forget her kindness and how she helped me to not be shy," says Fannie. Another person who had a profound influence in Fannie's life was James Hatcher, director of Town and Gown Theater in Birmingham, Alabama. He helped her blossom as an actress. Those unsung heroes helped set the tone for Fannie's future.

Fannie shares this story: "One evening after a theater performance we were asked to stay a little longer so people could get autographs and photos. I recall being in such a rush. I was going to try to head out to a party and not stay. All of a sudden I saw this beautiful young girl in a white dress with her mom smiling at me; you see, she was crippled and it took her longer to get backstage. She was so excited to meet me and have her picture made with me. I recall the incident as the changing moment in how I viewed the fans. I know now we all can be someone's hero and one person can make a difference in our lives. I want to remind people of just how wonderful they are. Most people find their pinnacle in high school or college and the rest is downhill. I believe life should continuously get better if we will only have the courage to believe in ourselves," says Fannie.

Fannie loves people but she also loves her downtime, like sitting at home and having a simple southern dinner in front of the television.

If you have never had the privilege of hearing Fannie as a speaker, you should treat yourself soon. Fannie Flagg has come a long way from Town and Gown Theater in Birmingham, Alabama, to New York City, as a writer/actress for *Candid Camera* and now a writer on the *New York Times* bestseller list. Yet life has come full circle for Fannie, because she loves to come to Alabama to a calmer life to live simpler with those who love and support her the most.

fun

Burger Baked Beans

1   pound ground chuck
4   strips of bacon, cut into small pieces
1   medium onion, chopped
2   1-pound cans of pork 'n beans
½   cup catsup
½   cup sorghum
½   teaspoon dry mustard
1   tablespoon Worcestershire sauce

Brown ground beef. Fry bacon. Combine all ingredients; pour into baking dish and bake at 375° for 30 minutes.

Julie Bolton, Madison, Tennessee

Sweet & Sour Slaw

Slaw:
1   medium head cabbage, shredded
1   large onion, thinly sliced
¾   cup sugar

Dressing:
1   tablespoon salt
1   teaspoon dry mustard
1   teaspoon celery seed
2   teaspoons sugar
¾   cup light vegetable oil
1   cup white vinegar

Slaw: Alternate layers of cabbage and onion in bowl. Sprinkle with the sugar. Dressing: Combine dry ingredients in saucepan and stir in oil and vinegar. Bring to boil; pour hot dressing over slaw. Chill at least 4 hours. Store in refrigerator. Lasts indefinitely.

Serves 10

Judy Sargent, Birmingham, Alabama

Cancer survivor and Alabama Senator Roger Bedford enjoying the TNN shoot with Edie at Buddy Killen's estate

Savory Sweet Potato Casserole

3   cups cooked sweet potatoes

Mix with:

1   egg, beaten

½   cup evaporated milk

⅓   cup butter

¼   teaspoon salt

½   cup sugar

1   teaspoon vanilla

½   cup evaporated milk

1   teaspoon cinnamon

Cinnamon topping:

½   cup brown sugar

⅓   cup flour

⅓   cup melted butter

1   cup flaked coconut

1   cup pecans

Bake 350° for 30 to 40 minutes.

Patty Barrett, Gadsden, Alabama

Gerry's Carrots with Canadian Bacon

3   tablespoons butter or margarine

3   cups fresh carrots, sliced

    Salt and pepper

3   slices bacon, cooked and crumbled

2   tablespoons parsley, chopped

In a large skillet, melt the butter and sauté the carrots until they are tender. Add the salt and pepper, bacon, and parsley. Toss together and simmer for a few minutes. Serve warm.

Serves 4

Gerry Mitchell, Cobourg, Ontario

Rockin' Red Cabbage

¼   cup (½ stick) butter

4   cups red cabbage, shredded

2   tart apples, thinly sliced

½   cup water

¼   cup fresh lemon juice

½   teaspoon caraway seeds

½   teaspoon salt

⅛   teaspoon pepper

In a 2-quart saucepan with a cover, melt the butter. Add the remaining ingredients and stir lightly. Cover and cook 10 to 15 minutes, or until the cabbage is just tender.

Serves 6

Helen and Doyle Hood, Nashville, Tennessee

kidding around with actress and breast cancer survivor Ann Jillian at her home in Los Angeles, 1988

How to Conduct a Monthly Breast Self-Exam

In the shower: Raise one arm and with fingers flat, touch every part of each breast, gently feeling for a lump or thickening. Use your right hand to examine your left breast and your left hand for your right breast.

Before a mirror: With arms at your sides, then raised above your head, look carefully for changes in the size, shape and contour of each breast. Look for puckering, dimpling, or changes in skin texture. Gently squeeze both nipples and look for discharge.

Lying down: Place a towel or pillow under your right shoulder and your right hand behind your head. Examine your right breast with your left hand. Fingers flat, press gently in small circles, starting at the outermost top edge of your breast and spiraling in toward the nipple. Examine every part of the breast and repeat with the other. With your arm resting on a firm surface, use the same circular motion to examine the underarm area. This is breast tissue, too.

Brighten Up Your Day with Broccoli Casserole

2   10-ounce packages frozen broccoli, chopped

1   10¾-ounce can Cream of Mushroom soup

1   cup mayonnaise

    Salt and pepper to taste

1   small onion, chopped

1   cup Cheddar cheese, grated

½   cup (1 stick) butter or margarine

1   14-ounce package herb stuffing mix

Preheat the oven to 350°. Cook the broccoli according to the package directions. Drain and place in a casserole dish. Mix in the soup, mayonnaise, salt and pepper, and onion. Sprinkle with cheese. Mix the butter and stuffing mix and sprinkle over the top. Bake for 45 minutes.

Serves 6

Karen Bracket, Atlanta, Georgia

Sweet Potato Delight

10   medium-sized sweet potatoes

2   tablespoons vegetable oil

¾   cup butter or margarine

⅓   cup bourbon

½   teaspoon salt

½   cup walnuts or pecans, coarsely chopped

2   tablespoons butter or margarine

Preheat the oven to 350°. Wash the sweet potatoes well. Rub them with vegetable oil. Place the potatoes on a baking sheet and bake for 1 hour or until tender. Cool the potatoes to the touch. Remove the pulp.

In a large bowl, combine the pulp, butter or margarine, bourbon, and salt. Beat with an electric mixer until light and fluffy. Stir in the nuts, reserving 2 tablespoons for garnish. Spoon the potato mixture into a lightly greased 1-quart casserole dish. Dot with butter and sprinkle with the reserved nuts. Bake for 20 minutes.

Serves 8

Jackie Hacker Coleman, Highland, Indiana

Super-Duper Sweet Potato Casserole

3   cups cooked sweet
    potatoes
2   large eggs, slightly
    beaten
1   cup sugar
1½ teaspoons vanilla
    extract
1   cup frozen coconut
½   cup (1 stick) butter

Topping:

1   cup chopped walnuts
½   cup (1 stick) butter
1   cup firmly packed
    brown sugar
½   cup self-rising flour

Preheat the oven to 350°. In a large bowl, mix together the potatoes, eggs, sugar, vanilla, coconut, and butter. Pour into a large casserole dish and bake for 20 minutes.

While baking, in a large bowl combine the walnuts, ½ cup of butter, brown sugar, and flour. Remove the casserole from the oven when done and drizzle the topping mixture over it. Return the casserole to the oven and bake until the topping is brown. Be careful not to overbake, because the topping will be tough.

Serves 6

Marie Isbell, Sylacauga, Alabama

A Psalm of Life

Tell me not in mournful numbers,
Life is but an empty dream!
For the soul is dead that slumbers,
And things are not what they seem.

Life is real! Life is earnest!
And the grave is not its goal;
Dust thou are, to dust thou returnest,
Was not spoken of the soul.

Not enjoyment, and not sorrow,
Is our destined end or way;
But to act, that each tomorrow
Find us farther than today.

Art is long, and Time is fleeting,
And our hearts, though stout and brave,
Still, like muffled drums, are beating
Funeral marches to the grave.

In the world's broad field of battle,
In the bivouac of Life,
Be not like dumb, driven cattle!
Be a hero in the strife!

Trust no Future, howe'er pleasant!
Let the dead Past bury its dead!
Act—act in the living Present!
Heart within, and God o'erhead!

Lives of great men all remind us
We can make our lives sublime,
And, departing, leave behind us
Footprints on the sand of time;

Footprints, that perhaps another,
Sailing o'er life's solemn main,
A forlorn and shipwrecked brother,
Seeing, shall take heart again.

Let us then be up and doing,
With a heart for any fate;
Still achieving, still pursuing,
Learn to labor and to wait.

—Henry Wadsworth Longfellow

Baked Sweet Potato

Start with a sweet potato about the size of a man's fist. It it's larger than that, it will be grainy, and if it's too small, it will be stringy.

Wash and then bake the sweet potato in a moderately hot oven. If the oven is too hot the skin will dry out and that would be a tremendous loss since the skin is the best part of the potato.

When the potato is nice and soft, remove it from the oven, slit it down the middle, and literally saturate it with gobs of polyunsaturated margarine—if you need to watch your cholesterol like I do—otherwise, gob on the butter.

Make certain every inch of that sweet potato is bathed in butter or margarine. To add anything else amounts to sacrilege and you will ruin one of God's most magnificent foods, so please don't add *anything* else to that potato.

A true sweet potato connoisseur would never dream of eating one along with a meal. The baked sweet potato is to be enjoyed as a separate meal or as a dessert. Before you take the first bite, rinse your mouth with good, cold water so that those taste buds are alive and poppin'. The close your eyes for that first small bite of potato, and I can tell you, friend if you've never experienced the ecstasy of that moment, you're in for a *real* treat—it's absolutely magnificent!

Because my wife does not share my love, passion, and enthusiasm for the baked sweet potato, I know she is thinking only of me when she selects, washes, and bakes one. That's why I consider love to be a baked sweet potato. Yes, I believe that love is a long series of little things that you do for your mate for no reason at all except the best reason of them all—you love and want to please your mate. When you do those "little things," like baking a sweet potato, you are unselfishly saying I LOVE YOU! If you accept this idea, love and romance will be alive as long as the marriage exists—and the marriage will exist as long as you do.

Zig Ziglar,
author and motivational expert

The Ziglars—daughters Julie and Cindy, Zig, Edie, Ben Speer, and Zig's wife, Jean, at the Gaither's Family Fest in Gatlinburg, Tennessee

Jammin' Baked Beans

1	pound ground chuck
1	12-ounce package bacon, cut into 2-inch pieces
2	16-ounce cans pork 'n beans
2	16-ounce cans kidney beans
2	16-ounce cans Northern beans
¾	cup ketchup
¾	cup brown sugar
1	teaspoon mustard
1	teaspoon vinegar

In a skillet, brown the ground chuck and drain. Semi-fry the bacon and reserve some of the drippings. In a crock pot, combine all of the ingredients. Cook on low overnight.

Serves 10 to 12

Rebecca O'Shields, Jasper, Alabama

Ravishing Red Beans

1	pound dried red kidney beans
3	smoked pork or ham hocks
1	pound smoked pork sausage, cut into ½-inch slices
4	ribs celery, chopped
2	large onions, peeled and chopped
1	large green pepper, chopped
2	teaspoons minced garlic
3	bay leaves
½-1	teaspoon salt
½	teaspoon white pepper
1	teaspoon thyme
1	teaspoon oregano
1-2	teaspoons hot sauce
6	cups water

Rinse the beans in a colander under cold running water. Discard any debris or broken beans. Either cover and soak in cold water for 4 to 6 hours, or bring to a boil and allow to sit, covered, for 1 hour. Drain.

Bring the beans and ham hocks to a boil with 2 quarts of fresh water. Simmer covered for 1 hour then remove the ham hocks and drain the beans. When the ham hocks are cool enough to handle, remove the meat and discard the skin, fat, and bones.

While the beans are simmering, in a skillet, brown the sausage over medium heat. Remove the sausage with a slotted spoon and add the celery, onion, green pepper, and garlic to the skillet. Sauté until the onion is translucent. Place the beans, sausage, vegetables, ham meat, bay leaves, salt, pepper, thyme, oregano, and hot sauce in a saucepan with the 6 cups of water. Bring to a boil over medium heat, stirring occasionally, and cook for 45 to 60 minutes over low heat, stirring frequently, especially toward the end of the cooking time. The mixture should be thick and the beans should have started to break up.

Discard the bay leaves.

Serves 4 to 6

Edie Hand

Over the Rainbow Red Rice

4   strips bacon, diced

¼   pound link sausage, diced

1   medium onion, chopped

½   bell pepper, diced

1   rib celery, diced

1   15-ounce can tomato sauce, plus 2½ cans water

    Salt and pepper

1   tablespoon sugar

2½ cups converted rice

¼   cup (½ stick) butter

In a large pot, fry the bacon and sausage. Pour off the fat. Remove the meat and sauté the vegetables in the pot. Return the meat to the pot. Add the tomato sauce and the 2½ cans of water. Season with salt and pepper. Bring to a boil. Add the sugar and rice and cook for 45 minutes, covered. Add the butter. Serve with barbecued pork, fish, chicken, pork chops, or sausage.

Serves 6

Bucky Kinsaul, Dora, Alabama

Country Boy Black-Eyed Peas

1   12-ounce bag black-eyed peas

5   cups water

    Ham hock (from your local butcher)

    Pepper to taste

1   medium onion, chopped

Wash the beans in a colander. Soak them overnight in a bowl, just covered with water. Drain the water in the morning. Place the beans in a large pot with 5 cups of water. Drop in a ham hock. Sprinkle some pepper to taste. Bring the water to a boil and cook for 3 hours on low to medium heat. Check periodically to make sure the water does not cook out. With a large spoon, mash some beans in the pot to create an almost gravy-like effect. Serve with fresh chopped onions.

Serves 4 to 6

Country Boy Eddie, Warrior, Alabama

Pioneer Alabama broadcaster Country Boy Eddie Burns with Edie on his famous show's set

John Croyle's Attitude for Life

"And they shall be called oaks of righteousness, the
planting of the Lord, that He might be glorified."
Isaiah 61:3
༄

family

These divine words are the foundation upon which John Croyle, the founder of the Big Oak Ranches, has molded and shaped his attitude for life. John was raised as an only child from age 5, when a falling tombstone killed his 4-year-old sister during a funeral. This tragedy, however, triggered in Croyle a profound concern and compassion for other people. When John was older, he worked at a boys' camp in Lumberton, Mississippi. It was in those teen years that he felt that his Christian mission was to take care of kids who had nothing and absolutely no chance. John has dedicated his life to God, but that dedication has now spread like wildfire to the 1,300 children that he has taken in and called his own. But John's compassion for others is merely the icing on the cake. Sitting and talking with this wonderful man, it takes only seconds to see the loving heart with which God has blessed him. His story is amazing, and his attitude is simply unforgettable.

John's mouth transforms into a beaming smile as he begins, "I was in junior high school when a man came up to me, tugged on my sleeve and said, 'If you were to die right now where would you spend eternity?' I said, 'Mr., I don't know, I don't care, so get the heck out of my face!' I shoved that man away, but that man came back up and simply said, 'The Lord can give you peace.' Here I was in junior high school and I could choose any college in the country to go to for football or basketball, but I didn't have an answer to his question. So I went home that night and said, 'God, Jesus, Holy Ghost, whoever you are, just come in and change my life and I'll spend the rest of my life telling everybody you're exactly who you claim to be. If you don't, then I'll tell everyone you're a fake and a liar.' I'm really lucky he didn't toast me like a dog right then! The next morning I got up and was getting ready to play a big basketball tournament when I stubbed my toe. I ranted, raved, screamed, and cussed, but for the first time I realized it embarrassed somebody. Since that time, even from one embarrassing moment to another or in other times, He's guided me and directed me."

It was after John got saved that he began working at the boys' camp in Mississippi and changing lives. He remembers his experiences well.

"When I was nineteen, I met a boy whose mother was a

Big Oak Ranch Kids with John in center

family

prostitute and he was a bank and timekeeper for his mom. He would knock on the door and say, 'Mom, I've got a receipt and here's the money.' He handled his mom's business. I told the boy how to become a Christian and he came back one year later and told me word for word what I had shared with him the summer before. It was then that I realized I had been given a gift."

At this point in John's life, he was about to be faced with a very tough decision. By the time he was a senior at the University of Alabama, he was a standout defensive end about to complete his football career in 1974 under Coach Paul "Bear" Bryant. This outstanding career included three Southeastern Conference Championships, a National Championship in 1973, and Second Team All-American honors. He approached Bryant with a tough decision that would determine whether or not he would play professional football to fund his vision of using his gift and building a children's home.

John remembers, "I wanted to get the money from pro football and at that time I was playing football for Bear Bryant. Our record was 32 and 4 and we won the National Championship my senior year. Winning was understood, and I learned so much from him not just about winning in football, but in life. I have transferred many of his ideals into what we do. So, I sat down with him my senior year and said, 'Coach Bryant, I want to get the money from pro ball and start this home for children.' He simply said, 'Don't play pro ball unless you're willing to marry it.' And I wasn't willing to marry pro ball. It was one of the best things he did. He taught me many things. For example, one of the things he taught me is that if you are going to be committed to something, be committed to it. It's so simplistic, yet so true. Another saying I learned is that a man of experience is never at the mercy of a man

family

in an argument. People can tell me all day long that Bear didn't care about the kids, but I was there and I experienced it. The same principle holds true here. If someone ever said that about me, that kid can say, 'Uh, uh. I had breakfast with John this morning and I know he loves me.' Success quiets all critics, and we've been doing this now for 25 years. The only person that believed in this thing when it started was the girl I was dating, who is now my wife. She is the only one. We were able to start [building the first children's home] in August of '74."

It was then that the Big Oak Boys' Ranch was founded. The Big Oak Ranch is a private, non-profit organization that provides a quality home for children between the ages of 6 and 21 who have been abused, neglected, or are homeless. It was with the help of John's friends, such as Bryant and former teammate John Hannah ,that he first purchased 120 acres of land near Gadsden, Alabama. His vision began with a small farmhouse and five boys.

"We take no federal or state money, and everything we have is paid for. We don't build anything unless we have the money. The world is full of people that let someone else talk them out of dreams. When I started, I didn't have anyone to go see, and I didn't have a clue. I just knew what I had been put on earth to do."

His vision that started with a boys' ranch was soon to expand, however, after he witnessed a heart-breaking tragedy.

"Several years ago, we found a 12-year-old girl that had been attacked by her father while her mother held her down. They had to do an operation to put her insides back together. She was torn to pieces. I met the little girl through a social worker when I was walking down the hall of a nearby courthouse and I got to hold her. I went in the courtroom and said, 'Judge, let me have her and take her home.' He said, 'You've got a boys' ranch, it won't work.' I said, 'Let me take her home personally.' He said no, and I told him that if her father took her home he would kill her within six months. I was wrong. Three months later he did it again and killed her. I made a promise to God that when the time was right I would build a home for girls, so in '88 we founded the girls' ranch. It's now 325 acres and there are six homes there. We teach the girls how to look in the mirror and like what they see, because someone lied to them and told them they were junk.

"We've been very blessed. Now we have a boys' ranch, a girls' ranch, and a school."

John's dreams were not limited to the ranches, and he has worked to establish the Westbrook Christian School, which is a private non-denominational Christian school that provides a quality education in a Christian environment for not only the children at the Big Oak Ranches, but for children in the surrounding communities as well.

He said, "What's phenomenal is that you have the boys' ranch, the girls' ranch, and the school is directly in the middle, and it was founded way back in 1972! So, hello! Someone bigger is in charge here! What's so cool is that we [invited] all 1,300 kids that have lived with us since then back for a 25-year reunion."

John is a seed-planter for these young people, and he plants the seeds that dreams are made of within the hearts of these children. A prime example of this is illustrated in one of the 1,300 heartfelt stories that John has played a part in. "The day after one boy's 10 birthday his mother drove him up to our driveway, opened the door and told him to get out because the ranch was his new home. She looked at me and said, 'I want to take his sister home. She's not a problem. He's yours and he's really messed up.' And I looked at him and I told him the same four things I tell every kid. I said, 'I love you, I'll never lie to you, and I'll stick with you until you are grown, but if you do me wrong, I'll get you.' That clears the air of all confusion. By those four truths, you've given a child emotional support, truth, security, and boundaries that they are not to cross. It's simplistic but it works. Eight years later, he graduated valedictorian and had three opportunities for college—Harvard, Princeton and West Point. When he gave his valedictorian address, he thanked his biological mother and father, whom he said many had never seen. He said to them, 'Thank you that you loved me enough to leave me in the driveway of a stranger.' And then he said, 'Now I want to talk to my real mom and dad,' and he leaned over to his houseparents. We try to help people grow up."

John said that the measure of a man's quality is how far above himself he marries, and he also said that you reproduce what you are. If this is the case, then it explains why John's attitude for life is filled with not only love, compassion, and plenty of heartfelt quality, but why he also has a solid partner and friend in his wife and a legacy to carry on his foundation within his own two children. John is not just creating oaks. He is using his attitude for life to provide all those who know him with very unbreakable roots.

family

Brenda's Stuffed Yams

3   large yams
2   tablespoons of butter
¼   cup of hot cream
½   teaspoon of salt
1   tablespoon of dry
     sherry (I prefer Dry
     Sack)
     *You may add a little
     nutmeg and brown
     sugar if you like*

Preheat oven to 350°. Cut the yams lengthwise into halves. Scrape out most of the pulp. Mix butter, cream, salt, and dry sherry, and add to the pulp.

Beat the above ingredients with a fork until fluffy, then fill the shells.

Garnish with bread crumbs, dots of butter, and paprika.

Bake for 40 to 60 minutes, according to size of yams.

Brenda Russell, Beverly Hills, California,
songwriter, jazz singer, and
4-time Grammy award winner

Hackertown Corn Casserole

1   can Cream of Chicken
     soup
1   can mexican corn
1   box of Lipton's chicken
     flavored rice
1   bag of shredded cheese

Fix rice as directed of box. Mix Cream of Chicken soup and mexicorn and some of the cheese. When rice is ready, mix all of it together and stir. Top with cheese and bake in oven at 325° for 20 minutes.

Sue Blackburn Hardesty, Highland, Indiana,
Edie's Mom

My mom Sue Blackburn Hardesty

Hold on Butter Bean Casserole

1   can butter beans
1½ pounds hamburger
     meat
1   onion
1   package of Mexican
     Cornbread

Pour butter beans and juice in bottom of casserole dish. Cook hamburger meat, drain, and put on top of beans. Slice onion over meat. Mix cornbread and pour over the top of onions. Put in oven at 350° and bake until cornbread is done.

Sue Blackburn Hardesty, Highland, Indiana,
Edie's Mom

Three Day Cole Slaw

1   medium cabbage,
     shredded
1   medium onion,
     chopped
1   green pepper
1   small can pimento
½ cup honey or syrup
½ cup vinegar
½ cup cooking oil
2   teaspoons sugar
2   teaspoons salt

Chop cabbage, onion , pepper, and pimento, set aside. Combine other ingredients and bring to a hard boil. Pour hot mixture over chopped vegetables and mix well. Cover and set aside for 3 days without removing cover.

Roxie Kelley, Birmingham , Alabama

Edie and Gov. Don "taxing" over the next scene of "Holiday with Family and Friends"

Gourmet

Zesty Macaroni & Cheese

8   ounces macaroni
    noodles
1   pound sharp cheddar
    cheese
1   can mushroom soup
4   ounces sliced
    mushrooms and juice
1   cup mayonnaise
1/4 cup onion, chopped
1/4 cup green pepper,
    chopped
3   tablespoons melted
    butter
1   small package blue
    cheese
1 1/2 cups cracker crumbs

Cook and drain pasta. Mix with next six ingredients. Put in 2-quart casserole. Melt butter and blue cheese. Add cracker crumbs. Sprinkle on top of macaroni. May be frozen at this point if you wish. Must thaw before baking. Bake at 350° for 30 to 40 minutes.

Charlotte Crotsie, Jasper, Alabama

Fruit and Cheese Mold

1   cup dried apricots,
    diced (set aside 10
    apricots for garnish)
1/3 cup raisins, diced
1/3 cup sherry
2   cups brandy
1   8-ounce package cream
    cheese
1   8-ounce cheese, grated
1   stick butter, softened

Bring apricots, raisins, sherry, and brandy to a boil and simmer 2 or 3 minutes. Remove from heat. Cool.

Mix cheeses and butter together, stir in 2 tablespoons brandy and fruit mixture. Place in greased mold. Garnish mold with apricots, walnut halves, and top with 2 tablespoons chutney sauce with crackers.

Niles and Scottie Floyd, Florence, Alabama,
Eva Marie's

Heart Healthy

Southwestern Creamy Corn

1   tablespoon acceptable
     margarine
½   cup onion, finely
     chopped
½   cup red bell pepper,
     diced
¼   cup green chili peppers,
     diced
½   cup cream cheese
     (recipe follows)
¼   cup skim milk
½   teaspoon freshly
     ground black pepper
½   teaspoon chili powder
2   cups frozen no-salt-
     added whole-kernel
     corn
2   teaspoons fresh
     cilantro, finely chopped

Cream Cheese:
1   cup dry-curd low-fat
     cottage cheese
1   tablespoon acceptable
     margarine
2   teaspoons skim milk, if
     necessary

Process cheese and margarine in blender or the work bowl of a food processor fitted with a metal blade until smooth. If using blender, add skim milk as necessary for desired consistency.

Melt margarine in a nonstick skillet over medium-high heat. Add onion and bell pepper and sauté until onion is translucent. Add chili peppers, cream cheese, milk, black pepper, and chili powder. Cook until mixture is smooth. Stir in corn and reduce heat. Cook over low heat until corn is hot. Add cilantro and serve immediately.

Serves 6

a favorite of Edie Hand
as found in American Heart Association Cookbook:
5th Edition

I believe that people are as happy as they want to be or will allow themselves to be. Happiness is up to the individual, but as for me, I ask the Lord for two things every day. I ask the Lord to prevent me from doing anything that will hurt anyone and I ask Him to help me to do something that will help someone else in some way.

How to Ease Marital Strife

1. When a spouse makes a mistake, do not get mad at him/her for not doing something that he/she had no idea that he/she was expected to do.

2. Remember that people are not mind readers and that the perception of the two sexes is often totally different.

3. Never expect your spouse to think as you do and never assume that he/she knows what you expect out of him/her.

—Ben McKinnon, Birmingham, Alabama

Ben McKinnon, executive director, Alabama Broadcaster Association, and close friend.

Desserts

The Original Orange Cranberry Cake

1	cup cranberries
1/4	cup flour
2	cups flour
1	cup sugar
1	teaspoon salt
1	teaspoon soda
2	orange rinds, grated
1	cup buttermilk
2	eggs
3/4	cup salad oil
1	cup dates, chopped
1	cup nuts, chopped
1	cup orange juice
1	cup sugar

Wash and drain the cranberries and dredge with ¼ cup of flour and set aside. Mix flour, sugar, salt, soda, orange rinds, buttermilk, eggs, and salad oil. Fold in the floured cranberries along with the dates and nuts. Bake at 350° for 1 hour. While baking mix orange juice and sugar. Pour the mixture over cooling cakes.

Yvonne Watts, Jasper, Alabama

Lazy Hazy Hawaiian Fruit Salad

1	large can sliced peaches
1	large can bartlette pears
1	large can pineapple
1	large can black cherries
1	pound green seedless grapes
1	large can mandarin orange sections
3	bananas

Drain fruit overnight or for several hours. One-half hour before serving add bananas and black cherries. Dressing should be prepared and refrigerated overnight. Fold the dressing into the fruit mixture immediately before serving.

Juanita Cole, Forestdale, Alabama

Dressing:

1	pint sour cream
1/2	pint whipping cream
1/2	cup dry ginger ale
2	teaspoons lemon juice
	Sugar to taste
1/2	cup apricot nectar

Tennessee Treats

2   cups dark brown sugar
    (firmly packed)
2   whole eggs and 2 egg
    whites
2   tablespoons honey
1   teaspoon baking
    powder dissolved in $^1\!/_4$
    cup of boiling water
2   cups flour
$^1\!/_2$ teaspoon cinnamon
$^1\!/_8$ teaspoon allspice
$^1\!/_8$ teaspoon ground cloves
$^1\!/_2$ teaspoon salt
$^1\!/_2$ cup raisins
$^1\!/_2$ cup chopped dates
$^1\!/_2$ cup walnut pieces

Preheat oven to 350°. In a large mixing bowl, mix brown sugar and eggs. Add honey and stir. Add baking powder to water and mix. Add water to mixing bowl. Combine flour and spices and stir into mixture. Add remaining ingredients and stir.

Pour into greased 8" x 12" baking pan. Bake 350° for 30 to 40 minutes. To determine when treats are ready, insert toothpick. A nearly dry toothpick indicates they are done. Cut into squares while warm.

Tipper Gore

with Tipper Gore at the vice president's home, Washington, D.C., while attending a national convention for American Women in Radio and Television

Creating a Gingerbread House

Gather ingredients. All except the base are edible, but the icing is not very tasty! (This "recipe" makes one house.)

Icing:
1 pound confectioners sugar
2 egg whites
½ teaspoon cream of tartar
1 teaspoon water

Also needed:
1 sturdy paper plate (the base)
7 3-inch-square graham cracker
  cookies for the walls and roof
  Any candy to be used as deco-
  rations, such as peppermints,
  red hots, LifeSavers, etc.

1.   Make the icing, or "glue," by mixing sugar, egg whites, cream of tartar, and water. The mixture should be sticky and thick.

2.   Decorate all four walls while the cookies are lying flat.

3.   Put a glob of glue in a square shape on your base. Do not fill in the square, because this will hold your walls in place.

4.   Put a glob of glue on one end of one cookie. Stick two cookies together where they are glued, and place on top of one half of your base. Hold in place for one minute. Repeat for the next wall, and then the last one.

5.   While your walls are drying, start decorating each side of your roof while roof is lying flat. Spread glue over entire cookie, then glue small candies on roof top.

6.   Once roof is decorated, place glue across the top of the four walls and across the top of your roof. Gently place roof on top of two of the side walls, and hold in place for one minute.

7.   Cut two triangles out of the 7th cookie, and then trim the edges.

8.   Decorate the two triangles, while they are lying flat, and place glue all around the edges. Place gently in front and back of the roof where the two holes are.

9.   Decorate the base however you want. Gumdrops make great bushes!

—*Susann Montgomery-Clark*
adapted from
Step-by-Step Gingerbread House

fun food

making gingerbread houses with Susann Montgomery-Clark, Charlie Chase, and Lorianne Crook

Tantalizing Torte with Mystery

16 Ritz crackers
⅔ cup nuts, chopped
½ teaspoon baking
    powder
1 cup sugar
3 egg whites
1 teaspoon vanilla
1 large Cool Whip
1 plain Hershey bar,
    grated

Chop crackers and nuts together until quite fine. Combine baking powder and sugar. Beat egg whites until stiff; gradually add baking powder/sugar mixture. Fold in cracker/nut mixture all at once. Add vanilla. Pour into a lightly greased 9" round Pyrex dish. Bake at 350° for 25 to 30 minutes. Cool completely. Top with Cool Whip and chocolate shavings. Chill.

Rebecca O'Shields, Jasper, Alabama

Sour Cream Pound Cake

3 cup plain flour
¼ teaspoon soda
2 sticks margarine
3 cups sugar
6 eggs, separated
1 teaspoon vanilla
    flavoring
1 teaspoon lemon
    flavoring
1 cup sour cream

Sift flour with soda. Set aside. Cream margarine with sugar. Add egg yolks, one at a time, beating well. Gradually add flour mixture and flavorings. Beat well. Add sour cream and mix to blend.

In separate mixing bowl, beat egg whites until stiff. Fold into batter, gently. Bake in greased and floured 10" tube pan at 325° for 1 to 1½ hours. (Check for doneness with toothpick.) Do not overbake.

Rebecca O'Shields, Jasper, Alabama

Congressman's Chocolate Croutons on the House

Cut fairly thick slices of white bread (crusts removed) into strips, tiny disks, or stars, whatever you like. Fry these very slowly in butter or margarine until golden brown on both sides. Transfer to cookie sheets and dry thoroughly in a slow oven (250°). When cold, dip into melted chocolate until completely coated and place on waxed paper to dry. I like ¾ sweet to ¼ unsweetened chocolate for the coating, but if you like sweeter chocolate adjust accordingly. Before the coating operation, better try one for crispness, but don't eat them all. They are even better with the chocolate on. Pass these and they will go faster then cookies or candy.

Mrs. Tom Bevill, Jasper, Alabama,
wife of former Alabama Congressman Tom Bevill

Superbly Moist Apple Cake

3   eggs
1¼ cups oil
2   cups sugar
2½ cups self-rising flour
2   medium apples, peeled
    and chopped
1   cup coconut
1   cup nuts, chopped
½   stick butter
½   cup brown sugar
⅓   cup milk

Blend eggs, oil, and sugar until creamy. Add flour slowly; blend well. Fold in apples, coconut, and nuts. Pour into greased and floured tube pan. Bake in 350° oven for 1 hour. Cool about 30 minutes before removing from pan. In saucepan, mix together butter, brown sugar, and milk. Boil for 3 minutes. Pour over warm cake.

Cathy Nichols, Jasper, Alabama

Betty's Wonderful Fruitcake (A Must Try!)

½   pound candied red
    cherries
½   pound candied green
    cherries
1   pound candied
    pineapple wedges
1   pound pitted dates
1   pound pecan halves
4   ounces of candied
    citrus
1   14-ounce bag coconut
2   cans Eagle brand milk
3   tablespoons self rising
    flour

Dice cherries, pineapple wedges, and dates. Add citrus, pecan halves and coconut. Mix well. Sprinkle over mixture. Pour Eagle brand over fruit mixture into well greased and floured tube pan. Bake at 300° for 1 hour and 30 minutes. Let cool for 30 minutes.

Betty Weir Odom, Curry, Alabama

Years before God allows tragedy, deep hurt, or serious illness to happen in a Christian's life, He has already provided the strength, encouragement, love, and support needed to survive. With friends that He has chosen to be with us at that time and place, He represents His presence to us in our hours of need.

—Carlene Sowards, Germantown, Tennessee

Perky Peanut Butter Pie

Crust:
- 1¼ cups chocolate cookie crumbs (approximately 20 cookies)
- ¼ cup sugar
- ¼ cup butter or margarine, melted

Filling:
- 1 8-ounce package cream cheese, softened
- 1 cup creamy peanut butter
- 1 cup sugar
- 1 tablespoon butter or margarine, softened
- 1 teaspoon vanilla extract
- 1 cup heavy cream, whipped

  Grated chocolate or chocolate cookie crumbs

Combine crust ingredients press into a 9" pie plate. Bake at 375° for 10 minutes and cool. In a mixing bowl, beat cream cheese, peanut butter, sugar, butter, and vanilla until smooth. Fold in whipped cream. Gently spoon into crust. Garnish with chocolate or cookie crumbs if desired.

Stella Cordell, Empire, Alabama

future

Recipe for Life

Try to live as close to the Ten Commandments as possible. Enjoy life, enjoy others, enjoy yourself, and, above all, enjoy food.

—Dolly Parton

Suzy's Cookies

1/2	cup shortening
1/2	cup butter
2 1/2	cups brown sugar
2	eggs, lightly beaten
2 1/2	cups flour
1/2	teaspoon soda
1/4	teaspoon salt
1	pound pecans

Cream butter, shortening, and sugar. Add eggs, beat well. Sift dry ingredients and add to rest. Add nuts and place on greased cookie sheet. Cook 15 minutes or until brown.

Makes 5 dozen

Cindy Oates, South Lake, Texas
Cindy is Zig Ziglar's daughter and these cookies were a favorite of her late sister, Suzy

Divinity

3	cups sugar
1/2	cup white Karo
2/3	cup hot water

Stir the first three ingredients until all sugar is dissolved (meaning, no clumps of dry white sugar are visible)

Cook on high in microwave for 12 1/2 minutes. Do NOT stir.

2	egg whites
1/4	teaspoon salt
1/4	teaspoon vanilla
2	cups pecans, chopped

Mix these next four ingredients together. Beat with electric beater until whites stand up with firm points on end. Add a little at a time into cooked syrup. Beat for approximately 12 minutes or until mixture gets so thick that it is crawling up to the top of your beaters.

Add 2 cups pecans and turn out by tablespoon fulls onto wax paper.

Julie Z. Norman, Bedford, Texas

Dr. Daugherty's Attitude for Life

"There are three important E's in everyone's lives.
They are efficiency, effectiveness, and enthusiasm."

∾

Dr. Patrick Daugherty lives by the *E*'s above. While stating the words above is rather easy, living them is not, especially when your life has been a test of overcoming obstacles. Patrick Daugherty survived the obstacles he faced by learning to live his life through the qualities above, and now he works to share those three little words with others. You see, those are not just words to Patrick. They are the key ingredients in his special recipe for life.

Patrick grew up with strong teachers and a desire to help others that he says stemmed from his religious background. He says, "I was raised in a small community in the hills of Tennessee. I went to a family church and much of the teaching there was in the form of a list of commandments or in fire and brimstone. But through that, I saw a God of love. That realization was instrumental in a foundation for me that didn't take place until years later. I had no role models in high school and no desire to even finish high school or go to college."

Patrick had an accident while in high school and broke his hip. As a result, he walked with a limp. According to Patrick, that experience did not help his motivation or his self esteem, and it wasn't until three women came into his life that he changed and began to learn the value of the words above.

"It was my senior year and I was barely going to be able to graduate high school. My history teacher asked me where I was going to college and I told her that I was not going to go. She had noticed my limp and after questioning me about all of this, she told me that if I ever decided to go, just let her know and she could find me some funding. I was also offered disability at age 17, but I did not take it. Several months later, I met Rebecca, who would later become my wife. She always wanted to be a nurse and she accepted me for not being from a well-to-do family. She encouraged me to go to college, even

friends

though I had failed every course but one in school the year before. So, I thought back to the history teacher and got in touch with her. Through the Tennessee Department of Vocational Rehabilitation, she arranged to have my education paid for."

Patrick began attending Lee College (now Lee University) in Tennessee and it was there that he met the third influential woman, who was the chairperson of the science department at Lee.

He said, "I thought I would flunk out of college and marry Rebecca, who wanted to finish her career, but the chairperson of the science department said she saw potential in me and offered me encouragement. She improved my self-image and made me sense that I could accomplish things. So in nine months, I met three very influential women. I was taught through them, and my education at Lee, a lot of patience and acceptance of those different than me. Here I was, originally at the bottom of my graduating class of over 400, and then I was the first one to graduate college in 3 years. It was during that time that I prayed for efficiency and wise use of my time, effectiveness and being able to use what I had, and enthusiasm about being excited about what was before me. Those *E*'s are very important. Later I found that the word enthusiasm means 'filled with God.' When you have love, forgiveness, grace, and a self-image based on who you are and not what you do, it becomes contagious and you want to give it to someone else. Statistically, I never should have been the first in my class to graduate."

Patrick went on from Lee to earn a Ph.D. in biochemistry and radiation biology at the University of Tennessee in Knoxville. He then began working at Oakridge National Lab. While working there he had to work with cancer-causing drugs and chemicals, which fascinated him and gave him the desire to learn about cancer and how it grows and develops. He then decided to go to the University of Alabama at Birmingham to attend medical school. He became an oncologist and now has offices in Florence and Muscle Shoals,

friends

Alabama. Patrick's style with his patients exemplifies his practice of the three *E*'s. It is his style that makes him loved by all of his patients.

Says Patrick, "I was accepted and received a lot of encouragement to practice. People ask me why I wanted to work in the field of oncology, where my patients are going to die. Well, I tell them that the attitude is everything. Sometimes the last month a person lives may be the most important one, and some even say that the diagnosis of cancer is the best thing that happened to them because it makes them stop and see what life is all about. What gives me the greatest satisfaction is seeing a patient with fear in their eyes because I can replace it with control, peace, and hope. You want to use every moment that you have every day to live life to its fullest. So many times we get so busy and active that we let activity replace productivity. When cancer gets your attention, you go back and look at life and start realizing who you love. Coincidence is God's way of remaining anonymous, but Christians see that it is His way of working. I see myself as one of the most fortunate individuals in the world. Only in America could I be given the opportunity that I have had with the background I have. People need to remember that we are all afraid to receive bad news, so we often justify not seeking medical attention. Remember that you are still in control and you exercise that by choosing to see a doctor."

Patrick says that patients should seek a doctor that looks at information and gives the patient options rather than just telling them what to do. He practices that himself, and it is reflected in his success. Some people are unsure how to measure success, but Dr. Daugherty measures it by his *E*'s, and how efficient, effective, and enthusiastic he is. Many may say that Patrick is just a doctor, but he doesn't just help those suffering with cancer. He changes their lives and brings them hope. As Patrick says . . . hope is therapeutic.

friends

Pineapple Casserole

1   large can chunk
     pineapple
½   cup sugar
3   tablespoons flour (self-
     rising)
1   stick margarine, melted
1   12-ounce package
     cheese, grated
⅔   cup pecans, chopped
1   sleeve Ritz crackers,
     crumbled

Mix pineapple, sugar, flour, cheese, and pecans. Spread cracker crumbs over top. Spread melted margarine over crumbs. Best served hot. Can be reheated. Cook for 30 to 40 minutes around 375°.

Florence Farris, Fayette, Alabama

Mom's Apple Pie

⅔   cup Crisco shortening
2   cups of plain flour
1   teaspoon salt
6-7 tablespoons cold water
3   cups medium apples,
     chopped
1   cup sugar
     Cinnamon to taste

Pie crust: Mix Crisco, flour, salt, and cold water in large bowl. Mix well by hand. Roll out on a floured surface. Makes top and bottom pie crust.

Mix the chopped apples, sugar, and cinnamon together. Put into the pie shell and place on the top cover. Pinch top and bottom crust together with fingers and make a "V" cut in top crust with small dashes around the "V". Bake at 350° until medium brown.

Joyce Roberts, Huntsville, Alabama

Old Fashion Pumpkin Roll

Filling:
¾   cup flour
½   cup sugar
3   eggs, beat well
⅔   cup pumpkin
Topping:
     Powdered sugar
     Cream cheese
     Butter
     Vanilla extract to taste
     Pecans, chopped

Mix all filling ingredients together. Spray a cookie sheet with a nonstick cooking spray and cover with a piece of wax paper. Spray wax paper with nonstick cooking spray. Pour filling over wax paper. Bake at 350° about 10 to 12 minutes. After baking, flip out on towel and roll up. Let cool. When cool, take it out of towel and lay out flat on foil. Mix together powdered sugar, cream cheese, butter and vanilla. Spread over entire cake. Sprinkle with pecans. Roll back up. Can be wrapped in foil and placed in freezer for later use.

Granny Ruby Hostness, Jasper, Alabama

Classical Chess Pie

4   eggs
2   cups sugar
1   cup butter or oleo
1   heaping tablespoon
    corn meal
    Nutmeg to taste

Mix all ingredients thoroughly and pour into an unbaked pie crust. Bake in a slow oven of 300° until done—about 1 hour.

Ben Speer, Nashville, Tennessee,
of the legendary gospel group, The Speer Family,
director of Ben Speer's Stamps-Baxter School of Music

Sensational Sour Cream Raisin Bars

2   cups raisins (stewed)
1   cup brown sugar
1   cup margarine
1¾   cups oatmeal
1   teaspoon baking soda
1¾   cups flour
3   eggs yolks
1½   cups sour cream
1   cup sugar
2½   tablespoons corn starch

Cook raisins in small amount of water for 10 minutes. Drain and cool. Cream sugar and margarine, add oatmeal, baking soda, and flour. Put ½ mixture in 9" x 13" pan and bake 7 minutes at 350°. Mix egg yolk, cream sugar, corn starch, and raisins, and cook until thick in sauce pan. Pour over baked crust. Crumble rest of oatmeal mixture on top. Bake 30 minutes at 350°.

Michelle Johnston, Chattanooga, Tennessee

Homestyle Banana Pudding Filling

1   cup sugar
3   heaping tablespoons
     self-rising flour
2   egg yolks
2½   cups sweet milk
     Bananas, sliced
     Vanilla wafers

In a skillet or saucepan, sift together the sugar and flour, making sure they are thoroughly mixed. In a measuring cup, beat egg yolks slightly and then finish filling the cup with milk. Add this liquid to the dry ingredients, stirring until sugar is somewhat dissolved. Add the remaining 1½ cups of milk. Cook the filling over medium heat, stirring continually, until it thickens to pudding consistency. Cool slightly, then add to your deep dish of sliced bananas and vanilla wafers. If you wish, the "leftover" egg whites can be used to make your favorite meringue.

Marguerite Kelley, Guin, Alabama

Starlight Mint Surprise Cookies

3¼   cups flour
1   teaspoon soda
½   teaspoon salt
½   cup butter
½   cup shortening
1   cup sugar
½   cup brown sugar,
      packed
2   eggs
2   tablespoons water
1   teaspoon vanilla
1   9½-ounce package
      chocolate mint wafers
      40-50 walnut halves

Sift together flour, soda, and salt. Cream together butter and shortening. Add sugars and mix well. Add eggs, vanilla, and water, and beat well. Blend in flour mixture, mix well. Shape 1 tablespoon of dough around a chocolate mint and place on a greased cookie sheet 2 inches apart. Top with a walnut half. Bake at 375° for 10 to 12 minutes.

Makes approximately 4½ dozen

Jackie Sutherland, San Francisco, California

Aunt Charlolle's Pepper Nuts

3   sticks butter
1½   cups sugar
2   eggs
5   cups flour
1   teaspoon black pepper
1   teaspoon baking
      powder

Cream together butter and sugar and add the eggs, 1 at a time, beating well. Add the flour, pepper, and baking powder. Roll in finger size rolls and chill. Slice in ½" slices. Bake until brown at 350°.

Rochelle Reed Brunson, Angleton, Texas

Make a Teacher Smile—Down Home Apple Dumplings

2   large apples
1   can crescent rolls
1   cup sugar
1   cup orange juice
1   stick butter

Peel, core, and quarter apples. Wrap apples with crescent rolls and put in an ungreased pan. Mix sugar, orange juice, and butter, and bring mixture to a boil and pour over apples. Bake 350° for 30 minutes or until golden brown.

Doris Shaneyfelt, Jasper, Alabama

Old-Fashion Southern Tea Cakes

2¼ cups sifted all-purpose
  flour
1 cup sugar
1½ teaspoons vanilla
  extract
2 teaspoons baking
  powder
¼ cup milk
1 egg, slightly beaten
¾ cup butter or
  margarine, melted

Preheat the oven to 350°. In a large bowl, mix all of the ingredients together until they are moist. Roll out the dough on a floured surface, and cut out to the desired size. Place the cakes on a greased baking sheet. Bake until done, depending on thickness.

Makes 2 dozen

I used to have these with Grandma Alice. We would eat them with a cup of hot tea with lemon and honey and pretend we were dining with the Queen. A little bit of London in rural Alabama!

Edie Hand

Microwave Peanut Brittle

1 cup sugar
½ cup white corn syrup
1 cup Planters Spanish
  peanuts
1 teaspoon butter
1 teaspoon vanilla
  extract
1 teaspoon baking soda

In 1½-quart microwavable casserole, stir sugar and syrup together. Microwave at high 4 minutes. Stir in peanuts. Microwave at high 3 to 5 minutes until light brown. Add butter and vanilla to syrup, blending well. Microwave at high 1 to 2 minutes more. Peanuts will be lightly browned and syrup very hot. Add baking soda and gently stir until light and foamy.

Pour mixture onto lightly greased cookie sheet or unbuttered nonstick coated cookie sheet. Let cool ½ to 1 hour. When cool, break into small pieces and store in airtight container.

Makes about 1 pound

Carlene Sowards, Germantown, Tennessee

Quick and Easy Dessert

1 can crushed pineapple,
  drained
1 can cherry pie filling
1 box dry cake mix of
  your choice
  Pecans
  Pats of butter

Spray cooking spray on an oblong pan. Add crushed pineapple and cherry pie filling in pan. This goes straight on the bottom of the pan. Then sprinkle on top of this mixture dry cake mix and layer pecans. Place pats of butter on top and cook 25 minutes at 350°.

Kathy Hope, Fort Payne, Alabama,
cousin of Randy Owen of the country group Alabama

Celebrate with Champagne Cake

1   box white cake mix
1   box pistachio instant
     pudding mix
½   cup oil
4   eggs
1   cup club soda
½   cup pecans, chopped
1   large can drained
     crushed pineapple
1   small jar chopped
     maraschino cherries

Icing:
1   box confectioners sugar
1   8-ounce cream cheese
1   stick margarine
1   cup nuts, chopped
6   ounces frozen coconut

Thoroughly mix first 5 ingredients. Stir in by hand the pecans, pineapple, and cherries. Pour into 3 layers. Bake at 350° for 20 minutes or until done. Cool completely.

Icing: Cream first 3 ingredients. Add nuts and coconut and spread over cool cake.

Jean B. Williams and JoAnn Richardson,
Jasper, Alabama

Heavenly Homemade Ice Cream

4   eggs, beaten
2   cups sugar
1   12-ounce can
     evaporated milk
1   14-ounce can
     sweetened condensed
     milk
1   pint heavy cream
2   tablespoons pure
     vanilla
     Whole milk

Beat eggs and sugar together and add other ingredients except whole milk. Pour into freezer and fill with whole milk to line indicated on freezer. Freezers differ according to manufacturer.

Variations:
    1 15¼-ounce can crushed pineapple
    1 cup orange juice
    2 bananas
Blend and add these ingredients to the freezer.
    After freezing, if desired, add crushed peppermint, crused peanut butter candy bars, or crushed chocolate cream cookies. Use your imagination for a favorite flavor.

Makes 1 gallon

Faye Speer, Nashville, Tennessee,
of the legendary gospel group, The Speer Family

Sweet Potato Delight

Filling:

6   medium sweet potatoes
³/₄ cup brown sugar
1¹/₂ cups white sugar
¹/₂ cup soft corn oil margarine
4   eggs
2   egg yolks
¹/₃ cup low fat evaporated milk
1   teaspoon rum flavoring
2   teaspoons vanilla flavoring

Chopped pecans
¹/₂ cup marshmallow cream
3   egg whites, stiffly beaten
¹/₄ teaspoon cream of tartar

Crust:

1¹/₂ boxes phyllo crust (at room
    temperature)
¹/₂ cup corn oil margarine
3   teaspoons vanilla flavoring

Wash sweet potatoes and pat dry; rub with oil or margarine. Bake in 450° oven for approximately 45 minutes to 1 hour or until done. Remove from oven, remove skin, and place pulp in mixing bowl. Begin mixing sweet potatoes. Add brown and white sugars. Combine well. Add corn oil margarine; mix well. Add low fat evaporated milk. Add eggs and egg yolk, one at a time; beat well after each addition. Add flavorings. Beat sweet potatoes well to form somewhat smooth consistency. Divide mixture into 2 equal portions, placing each in a bowl. Add marshmallow cream to one portion of sweet potato mixture, blend in well. Beat egg whites and cream of tartar until stiff. Add egg whites to the other portion, fold in thoroughly. Place both bowls in refrigerator and chill well before preparing crust.

Crust: Remove phyllo crust from box and unroll. On smooth surface or bread board, place one layer or phyllo dough and lightly brush with mixture or margarine and vanilla flavoring. Repeat by placing 5 more layers on board— lightly brush with margarine mixture before adding another layer. Cut four large (evenly divided) strips in layers of dough—follow directions on box to form medium size triangles (fold one corner of dough diagonally across to opposite edge to form a triangle). Cut triangle shaped dough and place in muffin tin. Repeat process until two triangles are in each muffin cup. Remove chilled mixture from refrigerator. Place ¼ cup sweet potato-marshmallow creme mixture in bottom of each muffin cup. Sprinkle with chopped nuts and then top with sweet potato-egg white mixture. Add a few nuts for garnish. Bake in oven for 15 to 18 minutes before removing from muffin pan. Serve warm or cool completely and garnish with whipped topping or drizzle caramel topping in plate and serve sweet potato delight on top of topping.

Maria Brown Ephraim, Birmingham, Alabama

Rockin' Red Raspberry Cream Cake

1   package yellow cake
    mix

Cake filling:

2   cartons of whipped
    cream

3   cups confectioners
    sugar

¼   teaspoon almond
    flavoring

1   jar red raspberry
    preserves (16-18
    ounces)

Frosting:

1   carton of whipping
    cream

2   cups confectioners
    sugar

¼   teaspoon almond
    flavoring

1-2 drops of red food
    coloring

Chocolate leaves:

    Rose leaves

    Chocolate squares

Bake cake in 8" cake pan according to instructions. Slice cake in half. Put in a plastic bowl so you can pull cake into form of bowl. I use long pieces of plastic wrap so I can tie together to form into a ball.

Whip 1 carton of whipping cream, 2 cups confectioners sugar, and ¼ teaspoon almond flavoring. Put first layer of cake into bottom of bowl. Spread ⅓ raspberry preserves over cake, top with ⅓ whipping cream. Repeat. Put last layer on top. Pull plastic wrap around cake to form dome on top of the cake. Tie plastic wrap and put into refrigerator or freezer to make firm.

To frost, whip 1 carton of whipping cream, 2 cups confectioners sugar, ¼ teaspoon almond flavoring, and 1 to 2 drops of red food coloring to make a light pink frosting. Frost to make round.

Chocolate leaves: Wash rose leaves—bigger leaves show a better imprint of veins on leaf. Melt chocolate squares over low heat. Apply melted chocolate on the back of leaf. Put in refrigerator until hard—15 to 20 minutes. Pull leaf off chocolate. If any part of the leaf is left pull it off. Decorate the cake. The more chocolate leaves, the prettier the cake.

Jody Schefano, Dora, Alabama

Perfect Peanut Butter Pie

½   cup peanut butter (I
    suggest Reese's brand
    because it is sweeter)

1   cup powdered sugar

1   8-ounce package cream
    cheese

½   cup condensed milk

1   medium whipped
    topping

1   pie shell, baked

Pour all ingredients into a large mixing bowl.
    Mix together until smooth.
    Pour into pie shell.
    Chill and serve.

Melissa Ray, St. Louis, Missouri

Jordanaires Best Chocolate Syrup Brownies

½ cup (1 stick) butter
1   cup sugar
3   eggs
    Dash salt
1   cup sifted all-purpose
    flour
¾ cup chocolate-flavored
    syrup
2   teaspoons vanilla
    extract
¾ cup walnuts or pecans,
    chopped

This is The Jordanaires' favorite recipe!

Preheat the oven to 350°. In a large bowl, cream together the butter, sugar, and eggs. Add the salt. Stir in the flour, mixing to blend well. Add the chocolate syrup, vanilla, and chopped nuts. Turn the mixture into a well-greased and lightly floured 9" square pan. Smooth the top. Bake for about 35 minutes or until a toothpick inserted near the center comes out clean.

Cool in the pan or on a wire rack but loosen at the edges first. Cut into squares. Garnish with pecans or walnut halves or dust with confectioners sugar.

Make 16 to 18 brownies

The Jordanaires, Nashville, Tennessee,
the legendary backup group for Elvis Presley

Pumpkin Cookies: A Cherished Family Tradition

This is a recipe my mother passed down to me. One of the first questions I hear from my family on Thanksgiving and Christmas is, "When are the pumpkin cookies going to be ready?" My daughter is carrying on the tradition and bakes these for her friends.

½ cup shortening
1   cup sugar
2   eggs
1   cup pumpkin puree
2   cups self-rising flour
2½ teaspoons cinnamon
¼ teaspoon ginger
½ teaspoon nutmeg
¼ teaspoon orange juice
½ cup nutmeats or dates,
    chopped
    Candy balls for tops

Cream shortening and sugar together until light and fluffy. Add eggs and beat well. Blend in pumpkin puree. Sift flour, baking powder, salt, and spices together. Stir into creamed mixture. Add nuts or dates. Drop by teaspoonfuls onto greased cookie sheet. Sprinkle tops with candy balls. Bake at 400° for 8 to 10 minutes or until lightly browned.

Susan Hargett, Belgreen, Alabama

Linc's Tarts

1   cup (2 sticks) butter or margarine, softened

1   cup sugar

1   teaspoon vanilla extract

1   whole egg, plus 1 egg yolk, well beaten

2¼ cups sifted all-purpose flour

1   egg white, slightly beaten

Toppings:

   Finely chopped pecans or walnuts

   Cinnamon sugar

   Colored sprinkles

Preheat the oven to 350°. In a mixing bowl, cream together the butter and the sugar. Add the vanilla, the whole egg, and the egg yolk, and beat until fluffy. Blend in the flour until it is thoroughly mixed. Chill the dough overnight.

Roll ¼ of the dough out thin on a lightly floured board. Cut into the desired shapes. Repeat with the remaining dough.

Place on ungreased baking sheets. Brush the tarts with egg whites and sprinkle with the suggested toppings. Bake for 10 to 12 minutes.

My mother and I make these for all of the holidays—using everything from hearts to Santa faces.

Makes 2 dozen

Linc Hand, Dora, Alabama,
Edie Hand's son
from The Presley Family & Friends Cookbook

these cookies give my son Linc "a boost!"

Marie's Killer Cheesecake

Filling:

3   8-ounce packages of
      cream cheese, softened

¾   cup sugar

3   eggs

1   teaspoon vanilla

Crust:

1   package graham
      crackers, crushed (I put
      the crackers in a large
      Zip-lock bag and let the
      kids crush them with a
      can, and they love it!)

3   tablespoons butter,
      melted

2   tablespoons sugar

Topping:

1   8-ounce carton sour
      cream

1   teaspoon sugar

1   tablespoon vanilla

Donny and Marie

Add sugar and melted butter to crumbs and press crust into a cheesecake pan. Bake crust for 10 minutes at 350°.

Combine softened cream cheese and sugar in a bowl. Add eggs, one at a time, and add vanilla.

Add filling to baked crust and bake for 1 hour at 300°. Remove from oven and let sit for 10 minutes. Then top with sour cream mixture and refrigerate for at least 3 hours. Garnish with strawberries or fruit of your choice. ENJOY!

Marie Osmond,
entertainer and co-host of The Donny & Marie Show

"Edie's recipe for life to replenish the spirit": When the crazies of life finally catch up with you, you have to detach and drift into a quiet place to replenish yourself. I have found that simple pleasure to pamper oneself is the best recipe. Relax with scented candles, draw a hot bath and add oils, then soak. Read a good book not related to work. Listen to soft music, sip sparkling water or a glass of wine, whatever helps you to unwind. Do it at least once a week. You deserve it!

Mama Jewel's Hello Dollys

2   sticks margarine or
    butter
1   box graham cracker
    crumbs, crushed
1   7-ounce package
    coconut
1   12-ounce package
    chocolate chips
1   12-ounce package
    butterscotch chips
2   cans sweetened
    condensed milk
1   cup chopped pecans

Melt butter or margarine (1 stick per pan) and use graham cracker crumbs to make bottom crust. Layer ½ package in both pans of coconut, chocolate chips, and butterscotch chips. Drizzle 1 can of condensed milk over ingredients. In each pan, sprinkle ½ cup of nuts on each pan. Bake at 350° for 30 minutes. Cool, cut, and enjoy!

These also freeze well in freezer containers!

Makes two 9" x 13" pans

Jewel Hester

The late Jewel Hester with daughter Judy Hester ("Bodi") and granddaughter Joy Beth.

Evelyn's 6-Flavor Pound Cake

6   eggs
1   teaspoon each vanilla,
    almond, orange,
    coconut, rum, and
    lemon flavoring
3   cups sugar
3   cups plain flour
1   teaspoon baking
    powder
2   sticks butter
1   cup sour cream

Add eggs, one at a time, beating after each egg. Add flavorings. Add dry ingredients alternately with butter and sour cream. Mix well. Pour into greased and floured tube pan. Bake in a 350° oven for 1½ hours. Cool.

May serve plain or drizzle with a glaze made of powdered sugar and lemon juice.

Bucky Kinsaul, Dora, Alabama

Yummy Rum Cake

1   cup pecans, chopped
1   butter golden cake mix
    or yellow cake mix
1   package vanilla instant
    pudding
½   cup rum
½   cup water
½   cup Crisco oil
4   eggs

Glaze:
1   cup sugar
1   stick butter
¼   cup rum
¼   cup water

Put nuts in bottom of greased and floured tube or Bundt pan. Mix all other ingredients and pour on top of pecans. Bake 1 hour at 325°.

For glaze: boil 3 minutes. Pour over cake while in pan. It will take 2 or 3 hours for all the glaze to soak into the cake. Remove from pan.

Jackie Parker, Jasper, Alabama

Blueberry Brunch Cake

1   cup all-purpose flour
⅓   cup sugar
2   teaspoons baking
    powder
½   teaspoon salt
1   egg
½   cup milk
⅓   cup vegetable oil
1   tablespoon lemon juice
1   cup fresh blueberries
⅓   cup sugar
¼   cup all purpose flour
¼   teaspoon ground
    cinnamon
½   cup pecans, chopped
2   tablespoons butter or
    margarine, softened

Combine first 4 ingredients in a medium bowl, and set aside.

Combine egg, milk, oil, and lemon juice; add to dry ingredients, mixing well. Pour batter into a greased 8" square baking pan; sprinkle with blueberries.

Combine remaining ingredients; sprinkle over blueberries. Bake at 350° for 40 minutes.

Makes about 9 servings

Suzanne Whitney, New York, New York

Sock It To Me Cake

1 package yellow cake mix (not butter)
¾ cup Crisco oil
½ cup sugar
2 teaspoons vanilla
4 eggs
1 6-ounce container sour cream

Topping:
2 teaspoons cinnamon
3 tablespoons light brown sugar
½ cup pecans, chopped

Glaze for cake:
2 tablespoons margarine
2 tablespoons milk
1 cup sifted powdered sugar
1 teaspoon vanilla

Mix all ingredients and blend with electric mixer on medium speed. Pour into 9" x 12" pan or tube pan, well greased.

Topping: Mix well and spoon on top of batter. Cut into batter with a knife. Bake for 30 to 40 minutes at 350°.

Glaze for cake: Mix all ingredients well. Spoon glaze on top of cooked cake while hot. Enjoy!

Vestal Goodman, Nashville, Tennessee

just finished the last "Recipe for Life" taping with country superstar Reba McEntir and Buddy Killen

Chocolate Doodad Cookies

My mother prepared these for me when I was growing up in northwest Alabama.

—*Edie Hand*

2 cups sugar
2 pounds cocoa
½ cup milk
½ cup peanut butter
½ cup oats

Boil sugar, cocoa, and milk for 3 minutes. Take off the heat and add the oats and peanut butter. Stir until thick and drop onto wax paper using a teaspoon. Let cool and serve.

Sue Blackburn Hardesty, Highland, Indiana, Edie's Mom

No-Bake Chocolate Oatmeal Cookies

They make your mouth water thinking about them.

3   cups of oats
2½ cups sugar
1   cup peanut butter
1   stick of butter or
    margarine
½   cup of milk
2   tablespoons cocoa
    powder

Mix the sugar and cocoa in a saucepan. Add the butter and milk and bring to a boil. Remove from heat. Add peanut butter and oats. Mix thoroughly. Drop spoonfuls onto wax paper and allow time to get firm at room temperature. Enjoy!

Mark Aldridge, Athens, Alabama

Coconut Pie

4   egg yolks
¾   cup sugar
2   heaping tablespoons
     cornstarch
1½   cup milk plus ½ cup
     Carnation milk
1   small can coconut
1   teaspoon vanilla
1   9-inch pie shell

Beat egg yolks. Mix sugar and cornstarch. Add to yolks; mix good with milk, vanilla, and coconut. Cook, stirring until thick. Pour into baked pie shell. Beat egg whites with a little cream of tartar until about half beat. Add 1 tablespoon sugar and beat until stiff peaks form. Put on pie. Add coconut. Brown at 350°.

Carolyn Thorn, Burnout, Alabama
(Edie's childhood community)

Blueberry Cream Pie

1   cup sugar
1   8-ounce container
    cream cheese
1   large container Cool
    Whip
1   teaspoon vanilla
4   bananas
1   pre-baked pie crust
1   can blueberry pie filling

Cream sugar and cheese; add Cool Whip and vanilla. Slice bananas in pie crust and pour filling on top. Chill. Top with blueberry pie filling.

Willodean Shewbart, Burnout, Alabama
(Edie's childhood community)

Homemade Brownies

6   tablespoons oil
1   cup sugar
2   eggs, slightly beaten
2   1-ounce squares
    chocolate, melted
½-¾ cup sifted all-purpose
    flour
½   teaspoon salt
1   teaspoon vanilla
    extract
¾   cup nuts, chopped

Preheat the oven to 325°. In a large bowl, stir together the oil, sugar, and eggs. Add the melted chocolate, flour, salt, and vanilla. Stir in the nuts and spread into a shallow, greased 8" pan. Bake for 20 to 25 minutes.

Makes 2 dozen

Kristi and Kayla Poss, Tuscumbia, Alabama
Edie's nieces

Sweethearts Kayla and Kristi

Hot Fudge Sauce

1   cup sugar
3   tablespoons plain flour
¼   cup butter
5   tablespoon cocoa
    (unsweetened)
1   cup milk

Mix sugar, flour, and cocoa well. Then add milk and butter. Cook over low heat until thick. Boil for 1 minute. Keep hot in double boiler. Great over ice cream.

David and Cathie Hope, Florence, Alabama,
University of North Alabama
Coffee High School

Edie's Strawberry Balls

1   can condensed milk
1   cup pecans
1   cup coconut
3   small packages
    strawberry Jell-O

Mix all ingredients except 1 package of Jell-O. Chill in refrigerator for 4 hours. Roll into balls and then blend with remaining package of dry Jell-O.

Edie Hand

Mama's Coconut Cake

2   cups sugar
1   cup butter
4   large eggs
1   cup buttermilk
3   cups sifted cake flour
3   teaspoons baking
     powder
1½ teaspoons vanilla

Icing:

2¼ cups sugar
3   egg whites
½   cup cold water
1½ teaspoons vanilla
12   ounces coconut, grated

Cream butter and sugar for 10 minutes. Add eggs and beat well. Mix dry ingredients alternately with buttermilk. Mix well and add the vanilla.

Bake in two or three 10" greased and floured pans at 325° for about 25 to 30 minutes.

For icing: mix all ingredients except vanilla and coconut. Cook in top of double boiler over high heat, beating continuously until stiff peaks form. Add vanilla and coconut.

Margie Thorn, Red Bay, Alabama

Several ingredients blended together create the perfect recipe for life. First and foremost, believe in God and in angels. Second, have a dream that you reach for and practice the Golden Rule. Third, be prepared and get a good night's sleep in order to have the energy to tackle your day. Next, exercise when possible, and strive to eliminate the word "worry" from your vocabulary. Finally, live every day like it was the last one, and love the life you live.

—Patty Barrett

Gourmet

Classic Boston Cream Pie

Cake:

1/2	cup shortening
1	cup sugar
2	eggs
1	teaspoon vanilla
1 1/4	cups unsifted all-purpose flour
1 1/2	teaspoons baking powder
1/4	teaspoon salt
3/4	cup milk

Filling:

1/3	cup sugar
2	tablespoons cornstarch
1 1/2	cups milk
2	egg yolks, slightly beaten
1	tablespoon butter
1	teaspoon vanilla

Glaze:

3	tablespoons water
2	tablespoons butter
3	tablespoons cocoa
1	cup confectioners sugar
1/2	teaspoon vanilla

Cake: Preheat oven to 350°. In medium bowl, cream shortening, sugar, eggs, and vanilla until light and fluffy. Combine dry ingredients; add alternately with milk to creamed mixture. Pour batter into a well-greased and floured 9" layer pan. Bake 30 to 35 minutes or until cake tester inserted in center comes out clean. Cool 10 minutes, remove from pan. Cool completely.

Filling: In a saucepan, combine sugar, cornstarch, milk, and egg yolks. Cook and stir over medium heat until mixture boils; boil and stir 1 minute. Remove from heat; blend in butter and vanilla. Cover and chill. Cut cake layer into 2 thin layers. Spread filling onto 1 cake layer. Top with remaining layers.

Glaze: In small saucepan, combine water and butter. Bring to full boil; remove from heat and immediately stir in cocoa. Beat in confectioners sugar and vanilla (whisk if necessary) until smooth; cool slightly. Pour onto top of cake, allowing some to drizzle down sides. Chill before serving.

Jody Schefano, Dora, Alabama

Old-Fashion Custard

1/3	cup sugar
2	tablespoons cornstarch
1 1/2	cups milk
2	egg yolks, slightly beaten
1	tablespoon butter
1	teaspoon vanilla

In a saucepan, combine sugar, cornstarch, milk, and egg yolks. Cook and stir over medium heat until mixture boils; boil and stir 1 minute. Remove from heat; blend in butter and vanilla. Cover and chill. Cut cake layer into 2 thin layers. Spread filling onto 1 cake layer. Top with remaining layers.

Edie Hand

Heart Tarts

1   recipe Heart Tart
    Pastry (see below)
1   recipe choice for filling
    About 3 cups fruit
1   recipe choice for glaze

Prepare Heart Tart Pastry; remove from pans and let cool.

Spoon desired filling evenly into pastry shells. Top with desired fruit: fresh strawberries, kiwi fruit, or grapes; thawed frozen raspberries, blueberries, or blackberries; or canned sliced peaches, apricot halves, or mandarin oranges. Brush glaze lightly over fruit. **Yield: 6 servings**

Heart Tart Pastry:

1½ cups all-purpose flour
½   teaspoon baking
    powder
½   teaspoon salt
¼   cup butter
¼   cup shortening
4-5 tablespoons milk

Combine flour, baking powder, and salt; cut in butter and shortening with pastry blender until mixture resembles coarse meal. Sprinkle milk evenly over surface; stir with a fork until dry ingredients are moistened. Shape dough into a ball; chill.

Divide dough into 6 equal portions. Roll one portion at a time on a lightly floured surface just larger than 3½" heart-shaped pans. Fit pastry gently into pans; trim edges as needed. Fold edges under, and flute. Repeat procedure with remaining pastry.

Prick bottom of pastries with a fork. Bake at 450° for 10 minutes or until pastries are lightly browned. Remove pastries to wire rack to cool. **Yield: six 3½" tarts**

Egg Custard Filling:

⅓   cup sugar
1   tablespoon all-purpose
    flour
1   egg
1   egg yolk
¾   cup milk
3   tablespoons butter or
    margarine
1   teaspoon vanilla
    extract

Combine sugar and flour in top of a double boiler; stir well. Add egg, egg yolk, and milk; beat well with a wire whisk. Cook over boiling water, stirring constantly, until smooth and thickened. Remove from heat; add butter and vanilla, stirring until butter melts. Place plastic wrap directly on top of pudding; chill thoroughly.

Yield: 1 cup

Jody Schefano, Dora, Alabama

Glazed Cheesecake

2	tablespoons graham cracker crumbs
1	16-ounce carton cream-style cottage cheese
2	8-ounce packages cream cheese, softened
1½	cups sugar
4	eggs, slightly beaten
1	16-ounce carton commercial sour cream
½	cup butter or margarine, melted
⅓	cup cornstarch
2	tablespoons lemon juice
1	teaspoon vanilla extract
	About 2 cups whole strawberries, washed and hulled
	Strawberry Glaze

Grease a 9" springform pan; dust generously with graham cracker crumbs. Combine cheeses; beat on high speed of electric mixer until smooth. Gradually add sugar, beating after each addition. Add eggs; beat well. Add next 5 ingredients; beat on low speed until mixture is smooth.

Pour batter into pan; bake at 325° for 1 hour and 10 minutes. Turn oven off; let cheesecake stand in oven 2 hours. Cool completely; cover and chill at least 4 hours. Arrange whole strawberries on top of cheesecake; drizzle with Strawberry Glaze. Chill thoroughly.

Yield: 10 to 12 servings

Edie Hand

Islands in the Stream

3	eggs, separated
⅔	cup sugar
2	heaping teaspoons flour
1	quart milk
1	teaspoon vanilla
	Nutmeg (optional)

Cream egg yolks with sugar and whip until smooth; add flour and mix well. Scald the milk, and when hot enough, add the cream mixture. Stir constantly 20 to 25 minutes until it thickens, remove from heat and add vanilla.

Boil some water. Whip egg whites and add to water until hardened. Remove with spatula and put on top of cream mixture. Sprinkle with nutmeg. Chill.

Dolly Parton,
Country music legend

Cheesecake with Glac'eed Berries

1   tablespoon unsalted
     butter, at room
     temperature
¼   pound blanched
     almonds, finely ground
3   8-ounce packages
     cream cheese
½   cup heavy cream
1½   cups sugar
4   eggs, slightly beaten
     Grated rind of 1 lemon
     Grated rind of 1 orange
1   tablespoon vanilla

Preheat oven to 325°. Butter pan and dust with ground almonds. In electric mixer, beat cream cheese, cream, and sugar until smooth. Add eggs and beat again. Mix in rinds and vanilla. Pour into prepared pan and place this pan in a larger pan. Pour boiling water into larger pan to come ⅔ up side of cake pan. Bake until firm, approximately 2 hours, adding more boiling water when necessary. Turn off oven, open door, and let cake sit until cooled. Invert onto platter. Garnish with strawberries.

Garnish:
1   pint glac'eed
     strawberries

Sugar glaze for strawberries:

2   cups sugar
½   cup water

Dissolve the sugar in the water in a heavy 1-quart saucepan, swirling the pan (do not use a spoon).

Set pan over medium heat and continue to swirl liquid until it becomes clear. Raise heat, cover, and bring to a rapid boil (the steam that condenses on the lid falls back into the syrup and keeps crystals from forming and prevents the glaze from becoming cloudy). Boil for about 3 minutes, uncover, and insert candy thermometer in the syrup. When the hard ball stage (265°) is reached, reduce flame to keep the syrup at that temperature. Dip strawberries in the syrup for just a second, just to cover, and put on a baking sheet which has been lightly oiled or sprayed with vegetable oil. Use a straight-sided pan 8" wide and 3" deep.

This is the richest, smoothest cheesecake ever!

Jody Schefano, Dora, Alabama

Charming Chocolate Souffle

2	tablespoons butter
2	tablespoons flour
¾	cup milk
	Pinch of salt
2	squares unsweetened chocolate
⅓	cup sugar
2	tablespoons cold coffee
½	teaspoon vanilla extract
3	egg yolks, lightly beaten
4	egg whites, stiffly beaten
	Whipped cream

In a saucepan, melt the butter, add the flour, and stir with a wire whisk until blended. Meanwhile, bring the milk to a boil and add all at once to the butter flour mixture, stirring vigorously with the whisk. Add the salt.

Melt the chocolate with the sugar and coffee over hot water. Stir the melted chocolate mixture into the sauce and add the vanilla. Beat in the egg yolks, one at a time, and cool.

Fold in the stiffly beaten egg whites and turn the mixture into a buttered 2-quart casserole sprinkled with sugar. Bake at 375° for 35 to 45 minutes, or until puffed and brown. Serve immediately with whipped cream.

Marlo Thomas, New York, New York,
actress and daughter of the famous Danny Thomas

Marlo Thomas and me!

attitudes

How's your attitude? Have you got an attitude? Of course you do. We all do. Whether it's positive or negative or just apathetic, we all have attitudes.

The important thing about our attitudes and why we should understand the one we have is that our attitude influences how we react to our world. Your personal attitude will determine whether you face the world head on, side stepping, or running away. Your attitude impacts on every aspect of your life. It affects us and the ones around us. We all know folks we like being around and those that we don't want to be around. More importantly, your day-in-day-out attitude can, over time, affect your physical, mental, and spiritual health. A change in your attitude will affect you personally and professionally. That is why it is important to know where your attitude is.

I am fortunate in that I have met many people over the years and learned a great deal about attitudes from them all. One wonderful person that I met was Marlo Thomas, the daughter of Danny Thomas and wife of Phil Donahue. She is a successful actress most known as *"That Girl."*

Marlo gave me a book several years ago called *Free to Be a Family.* I pulled that book out and looked at it again the other day. It reminded me of why I decided to write my inspirational cookbook. I just want to share with all of you just how big the world really is and yet how small our own little worlds can, at some times, be.

When times are good, the world isn't big enough to hold your energy. When adversity strikes and setbacks occur, then the world closes in on you. I have found that it is during these hard times that your real world is revealed to you through those that love you and are closest to your family. As Marlo Thomas says about finding the strength to thrive through her loss of her father Danny Thomas, "There's a spiritual connection that still goes on with him. He's still there. If that weren't true, it would be unbearable."

I agree with Marlo. To survive life's situations, it takes a certain type of attitude. It also takes knowing what your personal world really consists of—your family. Memories and stories of our lives are passed on from generation to generation. Your relationship to the world and your family depends on your attitude. Everything is connected.

I hope you enjoy my "Global History of Family and Friends." I have selected some of their stories and experiences to share with you in the hope that your attitude will be enlightened by hearing a little about others who are going through and have gone through life like you. I chose the cookbook as the vehicle to get these messages to you because down South, as I'm sure it is everywhere around the world, the sharing of the meal—the sitting down and breaking of bread—is the symbol of friendship understood by all.

Edie

attitudes

Heart Healthy

Guilt Free Dessert

1   package gelatin
¼   cup water
1   cup orange juice
1   small package lemon
     Jell-O (sugar free or
     regular)
2   8-ounce container non-
     fat lemon yogurt
1   8-ounce can mandarin
     oranges

Sprinkle gelatin over ¼ cup water in medium bowl
Let sit 2 minutes, until softened. Heat orange juice
in microwave until steaming. Add to gelatin in
bowl, stirring well. Add Jell-O and stir well until
well dissolved. Add yogurt and mix well, then
drained mandarin oranges, stirring gently. Chill
until set. Serve with a spoonful of whipped topping.

Denese Bramblette, Jasper, Alabama

Mommies Peach Cobbler

2   15-ounce cans peaches,
     pour off ½ of juice in
     each can
⅓   cup sugar
½   teaspoon cream of
     tartar
1   stick of butter
½   teaspoon cinnamon or
     to taste
½   teaspoon nutmeg
     Pinch salt

In a saucepan, mix peaches, sugar, and cream of
tartar. Bring to a boil; turn heat down to simmer.
Add butter, cinnamon; and nutmeg. Simmer for 10
to 15 minutes. Turn off the stove. Layer an oblong
glass dish with prepared crust then pour in the
peach mixture and dot with pats of butter. Cover
peach mixture with remaining crust and use a fork
to put holes in the crust to allow for the steam to
escape. If wished, you can put aluminum foil in
the bottom of the oven just in case their is over
flow . . . (optional with oven foilage).

Sandra Dorsey, California

Sandra Dorsey's Attitude for life

Life is about the journey, not the destination.

☙

This simple, yet profound, statement is just the beginning of the attitude that the past president of the American Women in Radio and Television organization, Sandra Dorsey, has maintained in following her recipe for life. Sandra is an extremely influential person not only in her role as the president of such a prestigious organization, but in the lives of about 200 children that she works with daily. One of those children is her daughter, Kellee, in whom she tries to instill her encouraging values and beliefs. Sandra interacts with the other 200 children in her job as the regional director of the Foundation for Minority Interest in Media. For Sandra, her jobs as an organization's past president, a single mother, and a mentor are merely challenges with which she welcomes and enjoys.

Sandra says, "My attitude is one of curiosity and chances.

Sandra Dorsey, past president, American Women in Radio and Television

friends

I love challenges. That is what keeps me going, and I love living on the edge. You can not go through life doing the same things and meeting the same people. Dare to take chances, live your life, then be willing to share with others what you have learned."

Sandra has unfortunately lost most of her family over the past 15 years. She has taken her losses, however, and turned them into a newfound attitude for living. "Because I've lost my whole family, it's helped me to realize that life is short and tomorrow is not promised to me. So, I need to take every moment and make it happen. I've done that in every phase of my life by trying to make each day different, and I try to teach that to my daughter."

Being in such prominent positions is a valuable tool that Sandra has learned to use in very positive ways. She says, "Being at the top is important to me, because I can really make a difference from that position. That is why I do what I do. Every day with my job at the foundation, I know I am giving those kids an opportunity that they would never, ever get." Many people may wonder where Sandra gets her energy and drive to succeed in so many areas, but her answer is a simple one. She credits her mother with the wisdom behind her strength. "I got my drive from my mother. She always said, 'You're going to fall in life. Get used to it. You're going to make mistakes, so get used to it. When you fall, pick yourself up with style and grace—every time. There are falls throughout life in which we may draw strength. Believe that you will rise each time.' It's my belief that in knowing that I can, that helps me get back up again. I can meet any challenge that comes my way. I have a lot of faith and I know God walks with me and that his angels are all around me."

She says, "We need to teach our children how to truly love themselves. We get so caught up in magazines, television shows, fashion models, and the pretty people. We forget to teach our children to learn the skills to love themselves, to be able to share, and to have empathy for others. You cannot love yourself if you do not have empathy for others."

Throughout her path of life, Sandra has come into contact with many people that have shaped and added to her attitude for life. "Life is about the journey, not the destination. It's not about where I want to go, but about the road that takes me there and the people I meet along the way that guide me. This is also God's plan, not mine. The phrase 'let go and let God' is absolutely true. For example, there has been no other president of AWRT that has had the same mission for both of their jobs. American Women in Radio and Television's mission 'is to advance the impact of women in the electronic media and allied fields, by educating, advocating and acting as a resource to our members and the industry.' The mission of the Foundation for Minority Interest in Media is the same, but also includes minorities. All I know is, I have them both, and how I got both of them is God's blessing."

It is simple yet profound. Sandra's life may not be about destination, but one thing is abundantly clear. The journey she is taking to get there has not only shaped her attitude for life, but has made a difference in the attitudes of others. That is the most wonderful journey.

friends

Quick and Easy Cheese Cake Dip

1   8-ounce package cream cheese (cheesecake flavor)

1   small jar blueberry jam (or any flavor jam)

1   box Vanilla Wafers

Soften cream cheese on small platter, top with jam, surround with Vanilla Wafers.

Nancy Logan
with BMI in Los Angeles
national president, American Women in
Radio and Television

*I*t was June 4, 1997, Washington, D.C., two days before my 53rd birthday. I was diagnosed with breast cancer. Prior to this shocking event, my father had passed away the previous August in Tulsa, Oklahoma. Several days after his death, in a freak accident, I managed to twist my left shoulder, which resulted in surgery several months later. This surgery took place at a sports medicine hospital located in Birmingham, Alabama. I immediately began physical therapy to restore range-of-motion and healing. Weeks later, the therapy was not effective and required another trip to Birmingham for surgery to release a "frozen shoulder." Of course, more physical therapy was required to avoid re-occurrence of "frozen shoulder." After several grueling weeks of physical therapy, I began to notice a feeling in my left breast that did not feel just right. I thought it may be just the left side strain due to physical therapy (God works in mysterious ways). As a precaution, I subjected myself to a mammogram four months prior to my regularly scheduled annual appointment. (I have always been one to do breast examinations on a regular basis). That June 4, as you may well imagine, was a devastating day. Immediate medical intervention was once again required. My husband, Larry, is a hospital administrator. He researched the best breast cancer programs in the Maryland and Washington, D.C., areas. Through recommendations from a number of his physician colleagues, we settled on a superb program at the George Washington University Breast Center. In the following days, localiza-

tion biopsies and numerous other painful diagnostic tests were administered. This resulted in a lumpectomy (partial mastectomy) and removal of 15 lymph nodes (although only 1 revealed involvement). About three weeks of recovery was required after surgical procedures.

It was then time to return to the George Washington Breast Center to visit my medical oncologist. While my first blood screenings were being run, the medical oncologist spoke to my husband privately. He informed him, had I not felt unusual sensitivity four months prior to my scheduled mammogram, I would have died before Christmas. (Again, God works in mysterious ways).

D-Day with Hope

The oncologist gave me the option of Tomoxifin or chemotherapy treatment. I informed him that I wanted the most aggressive treatment possible for best assurance of no re-occurrence. I was physically strong and knew I would have to be emotionally very strong through chemotherapy. The first of six weekly treatments was not too bad. However, as treatments progressed, it became more and more emotionally and physically trying—loss of hair, weight gain, supplemental treatment for dropping blood cell counts, dental pain, sleep loss, and joint pain.

I remember asking my husband at the time of the second chemotherapy treatment if I could have a dog. Larry said to wait until treatments were completed. A dog would give me something to hope for. As it turned out, my daughter, Danielle, flew a Sheltie puppy from Birmingham to Washington, D.C., for me. This little dog (named "Hope") gave me joy and hope during my personal period of physical and emotional crisis—and continues to do so to this day.

Several weeks after chemotherapy was completed, six and a half weeks of daily radiation therapy took place. This daily ordeal left me completely—physically and emotionally—exhausted.

Over the months of chemotherapy and radiation therapy, my good friend Mak and Larry's good friend Steve were always there to help in anyway possible. Trips to the breast center and radiation therapy and calls to family and friends regularly were great support and emotionally uplifting.

One day prior to Christmas (1997), my daughter, son-in-law, and sister visited. Two days before Christmas, I experienced more severe pain. Rushing to the hospital once again, I had to have emergency surgery to remove my gall bladder. This surgery was successful and Christmas was wonderful.

After the holidays, my family returned home and, with Larry working daily, it was just me and Hope. Hope never left my side and she continues to be at my side everyday.

Now that all the surgeries and treatments are finished, I have experienced bouts of depression and weight loss. Once again, visiting my physician, he advised that Larry and I move back to Birmingham where I would feel more at home.

We have returned to Birmingham. The doctor was right. I'm eating properly, gaining weight, and feel about 90 percent recovered. There is a light at the end of the tunnel. I hope this story of my two year journey back to health will bring a better understanding to family and friends of cancer victims of what one endures on the road back to health. Had it not been for God, my husband, my family, friends, and "Hope," I am certain I would not be here today.

In God's Love,
D-Day Presto
(as told to Edie Hand)

Epilogue

The first time I met Nancy Brinker, I was attending a "sisters" luncheon in Birmingham, Alabama. Just the fact that there was a foundation that not only raised money for breast cancer research, but also celebrated "life" for cancer survivors drew me in immediately. I was taken in by Nancy's charm and poise. However, I committed to donate portions of the proceeds of this book even before I met Nancy. Two friends of mine who are breast cancer survivors, Susann Montgomery-Clark and Carol Cauthen, shared with me the wonderful things the Susan G. Komen Breast Cancer Foundation was doing with their annual "Race for the Cure."

Then it hit me! Yes! This is where my passion is.

Founder of the Susan G. Komen Breast Cancer Foundation, Nancy Brinker

My grandmother Alice told me at a young age that I was destined to touch others lives. I never knew how, until now.

And just as Nancy Brinker made a promise to her sister Susan G. Komen to raise the level of cancer awareness, I also promise to help educate women to take better care of their bodies. If just one woman's life is prolonged, or any person, man or woman, who has experienced losses from cancer will be inspired to reach up a little higher and hold on a little tighter to that brass ring of life, then my work will be complete. God Bless.

Recipes for Life
a Cookbook for the Heart and Soul
www.recipesforlife.org

Recipes for Life inspires, encourages, and empowers women to healthy living by sharing the secrets of America's best known celebrities. In this inspirational cookbook, you catch a glance of what makes "home" with Edie's friends and family. It's *cookin' up attitudes and recipes for life* with friends like Marlo Thomas, Buddy Killen, Dr. Judy Kuriansky. The Queen of Gospel Music Vestal Goodman shares the recipe for her "sock-it-to-me" cake! Send your taste buds into a tailspin with Brenda Russell's stuffed yams, and TNN's David Hall's famous chili! Learn the kitchen secrets of Marie Osmond, Zig Ziglar, Fannie Flagg, Nancy Brinker and more.

For Edie Hand, *Recipe's for Life* reflects upon the joys and tragedies from her childhood growing up in rural Alabama, to life at Graceland as Elvis Presley's cousin, to adulthood as a cancer survivor. Her treasures in life are people. For this reason Edie Hand will donate a portion of the proceeds from the sale of her book to benefit The Susan G. Komen Breast Cancer Foundation.

Name _____

Address _____ Zip _____

Home Phone _____ Business Phone _____

Check/Money Order Number _____ E-mail address _____

Mastercard or VISA Number _____ expiration date _____

Mail order form to: Pelican Publishing Company, Inc.
P.O. Box 3110
Gretna, Louisiana 70054-3110
Or call: 1-800-843-1724
Or visit our Web sites: www.pelicanpub.com OR www.e-pelican.com

_____copies *Recipes for Life* @ $17.95 + $2.75 shipping/handling ($0.60 each additional copy)

For speaking engagements see www.ediehand.com

Coconut Babycakes

2   cups flour

2   cups sugar

1   teaspoon baking
     powder

1   teaspoon baking soda

1   teaspoon vanilla
     extract

1   cup shredded coconut

1   cup cooking oil
     (suggest Mazola canola
     oil)

4   eggs

Frosting:

¼   cup chopped favorite
     fruit or assorted fruits

⅛   cup shredded coconut

1   small container Lite
     Cool Whip

     Toasted almonds
     (optional)

In a bowl, combine flour, sugar, baking powder, baking soda, and vanilla. Add remaining ingredients. Beat with an electric mixer until combined. Pour into 2 greased and floured 9 x 1½ round cake pans. Bake at 350 degrees for 30 to 35 minutes until a toothpick inserted in the middle comes out clean. Cool on wire racks. Place a sheet of wax paper on work surface. Place the cakes on the wax paper. Using 3 graduated sizes of round cutters, cut the cooked cakes. You will have 3 layers for each of 2 cakes.

Before frosting, see "Circles of Wishes" information following.

For frosting: Add the fruit and coconut to the Cool Whip. Stir thoroughly to combine. Frost the cakes, stacking from the largest circle to the smallest.. If desired, sprinkle on almonds.

Yield: 2 cake rounds or 2 babycakes (the 3 graduated sizes would each be cut from 1 cake round).

CIRCLES OF WISHES™

Just Desserts for the Child in Everyone

Circles of wishes, Inc. ™ presents Renee Ricca's *Babycakes Collection*™.

Let your loved ones follow the ribbon to discover the real icing on the cake; a group of 14k gold or sterling silver heirloom collectable and branded jewelry collections featuring a color-coded gift card explaining the wishes, a silk moiré "wish-keeping" pouch, keep-sake tin, and gift bag to store your loved one's new-found treasures.

These gifts for every celebration in the calendar year have no age barriers, are perfect for baby showers, birthdays, bridal showers and every occasion. More sweetness comes from Edie Hand's "Recipes for Life ", a cookbook for the heart and soul published by Pelican Publishing Co. , with her favorite cooking, light recipe, heavenly coconut cake made with Mazola Canola Oil.

Hide your choice of wishes in rice paper, tied with a colored satin ribbon in our heavenly coconut cake before frosting. "Take your Wish" to find hidden inscriptions, engraved wish pendants, secret compartments, legends through flowers, carved star intaglios or scrolls of wishes for renewal, hope & courage. Wear them close to your heart and believe!

Babycakes™ -- because every cook knows the way to the heart is through something sweet.

The following women have partnered in the *Babycakes* ™ Circle.

Renee Ricca, designer for "*Circles of Wishes, Inc.*™ "is pleased to donate a portion of the proceeds to the Edie Hand Foundation.

Edie Hand, "Mom", cancer survivor, lecturer, radio/TV personality, and national spokesperson for bestfoods Mazola Canola Oil. A Portion of the proceeds from her new cookbook "Recipes for Life will benefit the Susan G. Komen Breast Cancer Foundation.

Jane Jarrell is a well-known food stylist and author of 25 books, including the "Love you can Touch" series.

The following stores carry the Babycakes Collection.

Silvertowne Jewelers
120 E. Union City Pike
Winchester, IN 47394
800-788-7481

Day's Jewelers
88 Main St.
Waterville, ME 04901
800-439-3297

Fortunoffs
70 Charles Lindbergh Blvd.
Uniondale, NY 11553
800-937-4376

The Goldsmith
919 McFarland Blvd.
Northport, AL 35476
205-333-1851

Lucas Jewelry
1825 S. Horner Blvd.
Sanford, NC 27330
919-774-3036

Cluxton's Jewelry
222 W. Market St.
Athens, AL 35611
800-326-4336

Mucklow's Fine Jewelry
552 Crosstown Rd.
Peachtree City, GA 30269
770-486-3400

Starnes Jewelry
127 W. Main St.
Albemarle, NC 28001
704-982-1013

South Miami Jewelers
7214 Red Rd.
South Miami, FL 33143
305-667-1898

M&M Jewelers
3419 Colonnade Pkwy. #100
Birmingham, AL 35243
205-970-0570

Ben Garelick Jewelers
5001 Transet Rd.
Williamsville, NY 14221
800-631-1586

Meigs Jewelry
110 N. Muskogee Ave.
Tahlequah, OK 74464
800-773-6233

Carroll's Jewelers
915 E. Las Olas Blvd.
Ft. Lauderdale, FL 33301
888-745-4367

I would like to share the "POWER of
a wish" with you. Untold possibilities
for "Change, Growth, and Miracles."

Believe

I dedicate this pendant to my special friend,
Edie Hand, "Cancer Survivor" and
Author of Recipes for Life.

Courage

TODAY, TOMORROW, FOREVER,
WEAR THIS CLOSE TO YOUR
HEART and BELIEVE.

Promise

Hope

Blessings,
Renee Ricca, Designer for
"Circles of Wishes, Inc." ™

Photograph by David Garvey

As a business owner, radio personality, actress, author, and mother, Edie Hand is the epitome of today's multidimensional woman. She understands the challenges women face in a society where their roles are changing every day. And she understands the issues they face, from health and beauty to career choices and family.

Edie has been a guest on both the radio and television talk-show circuits. She has appeared on "Sally Jesse Raphael," "Live with Regis and Kathie Lee," TNN, CNBC, and the Home Shopping Network. She has also appeared on "As the World Turns," as cohost of "Total Wellness for Women," with Dr. Judy Kuriansky, and as cohost of a television special with legendary songwriter/publisher Buddy Killen.

As a cousin of the late Elvis Presley, Edie has developed a following from fans and celebrities alike. She coauthored three books on Elvis with cousin Donna Presley Early. Edie also appeared on an Elvis special that aired live on Canada's CFCF cable network and recently coproduced a documentary called *Touched by Elvis*.

Edie is also a leader in education, from environmental concerns to health, finance, and other life issues. Her "Attitudes for Life" seminar series has a strong following throughout the United States. She is published by *Southern Living* and *Logger and Lumberman* magazines.

Edie is the author of *Recipes for Life: A Cookbook for the Heart and Soul with Edie & Friends*, and she is the national spokesperson for Bestfoods Mazola canola oil. Phone her at 205-648-8944 for appearances or speaking engagements. Please also visit her Web site: www.ediehand.com.